What Happened to Monday?

Dame Darlene Azar Rubinoff

To order additional copies of this book, contact:
Xlibris Corporation
1-888-795-4274
www.Xlibris.com
Orders@Xlibris.com
54409

What Happened to Monday?

Contents

In Gratitude

My heartfelt thanks to Hala Alameddine for her editing of
"What Happened To Monday?".

Author,
Dame Darlene Azar Rubinoff

DEDICATION

What Happened To Monday?

I want to dedicate What Happened To Monday? to my two Granddaughters Nickoel Azar Uhlmer and Gigi Hedlesten Ogelsby, for the love, attention inspiration they have brought into my life. God Bless and keep them always

Love
Author, Dame Darlene Azar Rubinoff

CHAPTER ONE

What Happened to Monday ?

Buena Vista could hear the quick steps of her granddaughter Nickoel descending the back stairs from her third floor bedroom. Vista knew that before the next clap of thunder, the usually self reliant Nickoel would be snuggled under the covers of her grandmother's bed. They had grown close through the years. Vista had always been there for her granddaughter. She wondered how much time she had left, and would it be quality time. There was so much she wanted to impart to her. Since her graduation from high school in Dublin, Ohio, Nickoel now lived with Vista in Houston, Texas. Was fate giving Vista this extra bit of time for Nickoel.

"Did you hear that Grandmother? The storm is right above us."

Grandmother Vista loved the fireworks of a good storm. Texas was a good place to witness fierce storms. The thunder of the storm vibrated through the big house. Vista and Nickoel were home alone. The lights dimmed and went out. The lightning must have hit a transformer near by.

"Do you want me to light the candles?" Vista asked.

"No! No! Don't leave me." Nickoel pleaded as she clung closer to her grandmother with each clap of thunder.

The streaks of lightning threw eerie shadows on the walls. "God is in his Heaven and all is right with the world." Vista said.

"Seems to me he is mighty angry with someone." Nickoel said hiding her head under the covers as the next bolt of lightning struck.

"It is spring and the farmers need rain."

"Yes. I know, but does God have to be so noisy about it?" The covers muffled Nickoel's words.

"Go to sleep little one. Grandmother will keep you safe."

Nickoel was nineteen, small of stature, just under five feet. Her usual calm and reserve made her seem much older. Except for storms, Nickoel was always in charge.

Vista could hear Kibbee, the Chow dog, whining. She too

Was afraid of the storm. Vista had Nickoel asleep in the crook of her arm. The flashes of lightning lit up the room

Causing Nickoel to look like a sleeping angel with her long blonde hair fanning out over the pillow. Kibbee would have to weather the storm alone. As Vista fell off to sleep her last prayer was that God would send a good man to love and protect her beautiful granddaughter after she was gone.

"You have been gone a long time Nickoel, Why?" Vista asked the next afternoon.

"You are joking Grandmother?" I just saw you at breakfast this morning."

"It always seems so long when you are away dear." Vista could not remember this morning or breakfast. Time seemed to run together at times and run away at other times. Was it part of growing old? She did not feel old. Sixty three was not so old. It was just this thing about time and places and other's birthdays. She seemed to lose it lately.

That evening as Nickoel settled down to watch television in Vista's room, Vista ventured, "I wonder what is on, on Monday night?"

"Grandmother this is Tuesday."

"Oh dear! What happened to Monday?"

"Don't you remember? We had a birthday party for Uncle Jim."

Vista could remember the party, it just seemed it was last week sometime. She would have to start writing down everything.

On Friday Jim, Vista's second son, came into the kitchen to ask Vista what month and day was John's birthday. Vista pretended not to hear. For the love of her she could not remember her first son's birthday.

"Did you hear me Mother? When is John's birthday? Is it the fifth or sixth of this month?"

Vista could not remember the present month. Texas was so different from Ohio. In Ohio she could check to see if the lilacs or the daffodils were in bloom from her kitchen window. All you had to check was the flowers, or the trees if they were bare or in bloom, or if it was snowing or raining and know exactly what month it was. She missed Ohio. She began to reminisce of her country home in Ohio, of the birds singing and the crickets chirping. She ignored Jim and the others in the kitchen having coffee and bustled about the kitchen doing nothing important.

"Mother!"

"Yes, dear."

"Mother, I think you are losing a few decimals of hearing. I will make an appointment for you this week with the Ear specialist."

"Mother, Jim is right. We all talk to you and you act as though you don't hear us." George said.

"I can go by myself. My hearing is fine, just fine." Vista said her voice escalating. "How are the children?"

"They are okay, they were just here Sunday to see you.

"I know, but they can get sick so quick when they are little."

"Mother they are teenagers and quite healthy judging from the weekly grocery bills."

It seemed to Vista it was just last week that she had rocked them to sleep.

"Has anyone seen the yellow pages for the telephone?" Nickoel interrupted.

Vista left the kitchen and headed for her bedroom and the large family Bible on her dressing table. She wrote down John's birthday on the palm of her hand and returned to the kitchen to tell Jim. "John's birthday is the fifth of May."

"Thanks Mother. Alma is going shopping tomorrow to buy a gift." Alma was Jim's wife.

Vista returned to her room. She wrote down the four remaining birthdays in the palm of her hand. She would have to remember not to stick her left hand in water until the family left.

Jim had accused her of having a hearing problem. A plan was forming in her mind. Tomorrow she would buy a hearing aid. She added that to the list of birthdays.

At Doctor Levi's office next day she pretended not to hear the high and low frequencies on the doctor's test, knowing he would prescribe a hearing aid for her.

"Oh! Mother how awful. I knew there was something wrong. You have been ignoring some of our questions lately. I'm so happy it was just your hearing. I mean . . . ." Evelyn her daughter said.

"Just my hearing!" Vista screamed.

"Mother turn down the volume." Evelyn said helping Vista adjust the hearing aid. "We were afraid you were getting . . ."

"Senile," Her mother added for her.

"No, Mother. I would never use that ugly word. I was going to say forgetful."

"Forgetful is like my grandmother Maggie, on my daddy's side. I remember when I was a little girl, everyone laughing at her. She would tell her sons they needed to go to the plumbers, when she meant barbers. Vista told other stories of grandmother Maggie. How she would have preferred to be called Maggie instead of Buena Vista. Great grandmother Maggie must have been a delightful person Nickoel thought as she listened to Vista tell how her grandmother had died of pneumonia in the nineteen twenties, after insisting her son Charlie takes her to the Circleville Pumpkin Show.

Vista's family always sat enthralled by her stories of the past. They said she should write a book. It would be wonderful if she had time to chronicle her childhood for her grandchildren before it was too late. It would be interesting for them to know of their ancestors' way of life. They should know of the uncles who went off to the wars and never came back, of the families that lived through the great depression. They should know how much things had changed in Vista's life time. About their Dutch ancestors who lived and farmed the Hocking County hills of southern Ohio. Vista wondered how much time she had left.

Maggie Koonrod was a Dutch woman who, according to her family, married beneath her. She married a poor immigrant German, Hiram Koonrod, who never learned to speak English.

Buena vista had carried the name of her mother's mother. Every first born girl for generations had carried the name, Buena

Vista. Buena Vista meant beautiful view in Dutch. Vista would have preferred the name of Maggie.

Grandmother Maggie had worn lipstick and loved parties and life. Grandmother Buena was a hard working farm woman and had a more severe attitude towards life. Vista had intended to change her name after her grandmother's death. Her grandmother lived into her seventies, by then it did not seem to be important anymore.

XXX

Harvest time in the Hocking Hills was a memorable occasion. The fall colors of brilliant reds and oranges filled the landscape. Orange pumpkins dotted the fields heralding the arrival of threshing time. In the twenties there would be just one threshing machine for a dozen farmers. That was before the days of credit buying. Several farmers got together and paid cash for their farm machinery and equipment. Then they took turns planting and harvesting each other's crops.

Before sun up the threshing machine would roll into the field to be harvested. Then the men were served a large breakfast of eggs, pork tenderloin, home fried potatoes, pork gravy, biscuits, and home made jellies. There was apple butter, that had been made early in the fall in big copper kettles, over an open fire, outside the smoke house. The wives had been in the big summer house kitchen long before dawn to prepare the breakfast.

At twelve o'clock a shrill whistle on the old steam machine would break the silence of the valley and echoed through the hills announcing that the men were leaving the field for dinner—On the farm in those days, the noonday meal was dinner and the evening meal was called supper.—Dinner was served in the summer house.

The summer house was a large kitchen built away from the main house. In winter the summer house was used as a smoke house to smoke and cure meats preserved for the harsh winters of southern Ohio.

The men were served first at a long table that would accommodate twenty. After the men were served the young children that were not yet in school were fed. Then the women ate leisurely as they watched the children at play. This was the only social life they had, except for church. It was here they exchanged stories of family and new recipes of *jam cake and shoo-fly pie.*

Vista could still picture in her minds' eye, her aunts bustling around the kitchen in their starched white aprons and flowered Dutch bonnets, their eyes sparkling with good health. They all had European features, turned up noses, rosy cheeks in milk white skin. There was no need for powder Their fresh rosy complexions imitated the simple life they lived. Everything seemed good in those days. The smells of fresh baked bread and pork tenderloins frying in an open pan stayed with Vista always.

Gradually the younger ones migrated to the city, to credit buying and later credit cards that grandmother Vista insisted was the ruination of the American way.

XXX

That evening as Vista was busy preparing dinner James put his arm around his mother. "I am glad you got the hearing aid Mother, I'm happy hearing was your only problem."

"What do you mean James?" Vista asked.

"Nothing Mother. There are a lot worse things then bad hearing."

Vista knew what James meant. She was getting more concerned at the things she was forgetting and at her loss of time. Soon she would have to check with the doctor.

It was fall and Vista had gone to Houston's Galleria at Post Oak and Westheimer to shop. As she left the shopping area, she could not remember where she had parked. She looked at her watch. Nickoel would be home from the office and would surely worry when she could not find her.

Vista went to the telephone, she could not remember her home number and it was unlisted. She decided to have a cup of coffee at McDonald. The number would come to her after a while, she was trying too hard.

Six thirty, seven, still Vista could not remember the number or where she left the car. The movie *Thelma and Louise* was playing across the way. By the time she came out she would remember.

It was nine thirty when Vista came out of the theater and remembered Nickoel's telephone number. She took out a ball point pen and wrote the number in the palm of her left hand. She would keep it there always.

"Grandmother! Where are you? I have been so worried. Why didn't you call?"

"I went to a movie and forgot the time. Now my car will not start." She lied. "Will you come and get me, please? I am close by the McDonald exit in the Galleria."

"Wait right there. I am on my way. Shall I bring someone to start the car?"

"No it's late. I would rather wait until tomorrow. James will pick it up for me." Vista hoped that by tomorrow she would remember where she had parked her silver and maroon Cadillac.

"Mother, where were you last night?" James asked as he drank his morning coffee.

"I had a date." Vista said playfully.

"That would not surprise me any. See you tonight. And do not go to any more risque movies. I heard about last night."

James was referring to 'Thelma and Louise' as he placed a wet kiss on her cheek. "I love you." It was reassuring to know her children cared. They would never have to feel guilty if anything ever happened to her, they declared their love every day. James reminded Vista of her deceased husband so much that sometimes she felt she was living her life over, like the rewinding of her favorite VCR. She was blessed to have children and grandchildren who loved and admired her. Would they still love her after she had forgotten them. She must do something quick about her forgetfulness, before it was too late. She never wanted to be a burden to her children.

"I will pick your car up later." James said, from the kitchen door.

The doctors here in Houston might inform her children of her illness. Vista was quite sure she had Alzheimer disease. She would go to San Francisco to consult with the old doctor who had once taken care of her husband, the Maestro.

The doorbell rang. It was eleven fifteen on a Monday morning. This was Monday, Vista reasoned. Vista was surprised to find her friend Sylvia at the door. "Sylvia how nice, you dropped by for coffee. I was just thinking about you, come in."

"You lie, you tell everyone you are thinking of them. I have known you too long. And you must be joking, you invited me for lunch. What are we having?"

"I will make us a salad."

"You better make enough for six guests." Sylvia said, the clanging of her large earrings matching the clanging of the armful of gold bracelets dangling from her wrists. Her black eyes snapped as she looked in the refrigerator to see what Vista had prepared for lunch. Sylvia was always organized and could not sympathize with others who were not. Sylvia lived alone. She had no one to interrupt her goings and doings.

"Six?" Vista exclaimed.

"Yes, you invited all of us the other night, when we were at intermission, at the Mozart concert."

"Oh, my goodness! I forgot. Why didn't you call me?"

"I did yesterday. Hurry, I'll help you make lunch. It's a good thing I came early. Really Vista, if I did not know better, I would swear you had Alzheimer."

"Sylvia. Shut up!"

Sylvia kept on talking. "Your trouble is you try to please too many people, your children, grandchildren and your church group. You take on too much responsibility. You know at our age we need to slow down. After sixty, it is down hill all the way."

"You are your usual ray of sunshine Sylvia. Guess I am sliding fast." Vista knew in her heart she would not trade places with her friend who talked too much because she was a lonely old woman.

"I am leaving for California tomorrow, I will rest there."

"San Francisco! I swear Vista you are always on the go. You just came back from that Christening in Ohio. Then Florida for the Bar Mitzvah. Your family does not expect you to be present at every occasion." Vista detected a hint of jealousy in Sylvia's tone.

"Of course they do, I'm not dead yet."

"I didn't mean to say anything to hurt you. I guess I get a little jealous sometimes. My life is so boring next to yours."

"I always ask you to join me, Sylvia."

"I know, but I always feel like an outsider. I wish I had a family like yours.

"You should have made the investment years ago. You didn't want to spoil your figure. You thought your husband would leave you. So he died young and here we are, both old and ugly, the way of all flesh. You can't stop the aging process. Hand me the scallions and chop faster."

"Now you have me rushing. I swear Vista you will never change."

Vista knew she was changing and it was not going to be a pleasant change. "Time and tide wait for no man, Sylvia." A worried look left Vista's face. She returned to her cheerful self, making all those around her feel good about themselves. Her cheerfulness had always been contagious.

The loud speaker called for the boarding of flight 711 to San Francisco. As Vista boarded the plane she looked back to see Nickoel throwing her a kiss. She had a sinking feeling in the pit of her stomach that some ominous thing was going to keep her from her beautiful granddaughter. As Vista soared through the clouds she kept reciting Nickoel's telephone number over and over to keep it indelible on her mind . . . 876-9707 . . . 876-9707 . . .

Maybe in San Francisco she would find a pill or a diet or a shot that would alleviate this damnable thing . . . 876-9707 . . . 876-9707.

CHAPTER TWO

San Francisco

Dolly and Vista were standing in line at Walden's book store, in downtown San Francisco, waiting for Bob Hope to autograph their copies of 'Don't Shoot, It's Only Me'.

"Remember we were together at the Ohio State Fair, when Dolores Hope requested that Daddy Rubinoff be brought back stage so they could have pictures taken with him?" Dolly, Vista's daughter asked.

"Yes, it will be good to see him again. I wonder if Dolores is with him?" Vista asked.

The line was very long. "I will take the car to Kearny street by my office and park, Mother. I don't want to get another parking ticket. You stay in line and I will be right back."

Vista got in the wrong line and had to wait for forty minutes all the time wondering what had happened to Dolly.

"To Vista Rubinoff, Mr. Hope. Do you remember I met you at the Ohio State Fair?. I am his widow." He starred at her. She suspected

Bob Hope was thinking of Dave's wife Mertice, whom he had met many times. "It's Good to hear the name Rubinoff again." He said, a quizzical expresion in his eyes.

"Is your wife with you?" Vista asked.

"No. She is visiting relatives in Idaho."

"You are in my husband's biography. I would like you to read it."

"Send it to my home in the Valley I would love to read it. All about the old vaudeville days I bet."

"Yes, it is, and the early movies of the thirties and forties and Hollywood and New York in those days."

The line was pressing forward. "Nice to see you again." A man behind her in line snapped a picture of Vista with Bob Hope. "Good luck with your new book." They shook hands and Vista went to find Dolly, disappointed that she had not been in the picture.

Vista could not understand what had detained Dolly. Kearny street was only a few blocks away.

Maybe she had expected her to walk the few blocks to her studio. Dolly's telephone was unlisted and Vista felt a little confused. She was not sure which way was Kearny street. If she asked someone and found the street, could she find Dolly's studio. Suppose she would not be there Vista reasoned. She would just have to wait here in front of the book store. Vista found a bench and sat down to wait. Evening was coming and the air was turning cool. Vista hoped her daughter would come soon. She hated wearing a big hat after sundown.

"Mother,. I was waiting at the studio for your call. I thought you must have gone to tea with the Hope's when I didn't hear from you."

Vista could not get angry. She could not tell Dolly that she could not remember her telephone number. "Let's go to the *Top Of The Mark* for dinner, then go to hear your friend Peter Minton at *L 'Etole.*" Dolly said.

Vista was chilled and angry more at herself and her forgetfulness than at her unsuspecting daughter.

Dinner was pleasant as they watched the city lights come on from their window table, atop Nob Hill. Dolly touched her hand. "I'm so sorry about this afternoon, Mother. I came back a few minutes later and I couldn't find you. Where did you go?"

"I was there, probably behind a book shelf in the long line."

"But Mother you were one of the first ones there."

"I know. I thought so too. But before I knew it, the crowd had shuffled around and I was way back in the line.

"I'm so sorry Mother, it won't happen again. Next time call right away."

"You shouldn't always assume things. You have a bad habit of doing that. Get the facts. Don't assume anything."

"Yes, Mother. Look! The lights on the *Bay Bridge* just came on."

"It's like a make believe land of lights, looking down from up here, isn't it?" Vista's question told Dolly that the misunderstanding of the afternoon was forgotten.

As they entered the lounge at *L'Etoile*, Peter Minton was at the piano. He saw them enter and went into his rendition of '*Hello Dolly*', from the Broadway show. Peter had been a friend of Vista's late husband. Musicians seem to appreciate each other's art.

Vista was remembering their last concert, when she and the Maestro had gone to Merschon Auditorium *at* Ohio State University to hear Izack Pearlman and meet with him at a reception that evening. Vista missed all those concerts and receptions. Maestro Rubinoff said that Izack Pearlman was the greatest Violinist who ever lived, possibly even greater than *Paganini,* the master of the violin and known for centuries as the greatest violinist who ever lived. Peter's voice brought Vista out of her revery. "I'm going to have to compose a song for you, Mrs. Rubinoff." Peter said as he pecked her on the cheek. "I have a present for you. Please stay for a while until my next break."

"I taped David's movie '*Thanks A Million*' with Dick Powell and Ann Dvorak. I remember you said you only had parts of it." Peter said as he joined them at the small table to talk of music and old times. Peter was quite young, but he was a collector of old records, music and memorabilia of the twenties. Dolly always enjoyed hearing them talk of the past.

As they readied for bed in Dolly's little studio apartment, Dolly asked ; "What do you have planned for tomorrow Mother? It is always so exciting to go out with you, you know so many interesting people."

"Just shopping, I need some fall clothes. It is much cooler here than I anticipated. It is not like Houston. You do your thing. I didn't tell you I was coming. I don't want to keep you from your work."

"You are still angry about this afternoon?"

"Nonsense. I would just like to take some time off to be alone, and enjoy myself shopping and meandering about the town and not worry about the time. I don't get much time for that at home. You understand?"

"Of course, Mother. I promised a friend I would ride down the coast to Carmel. We both want to paint the fog rolling in from the sea."

"You won't be back until the next day?"

"Would that be okay? Really Mother, I don't have to go."

"Of course. Go! Honey. I have been wanting to stay at the new Ritz Carlton. I will enjoy being by myself for a while. When you come back we will have 'High Tea' at the Ritz. Please, take all the time you want, I'm in no hurry. I will be here when you come back. We'll have another candle light dinner and watch the harbor lights come on. You wouldn't know it, but that's a very old song, *Harbor Lights*. We will have Peter Minton play it for us when you come back."

"Oh Mother, you are the best. I love you so very much. Don't go to *Fisherman's Wharf* until I come back. Promise! I want to go there with you. We will go to our old haunt *Sinbad's Restaurant.*"Vista was always happy when she knew her children were happy.

Vista had that same feeling in the pit of her stomach. A foreboding, ominous feeling, like when she left Nickoel at the airport in Houston.

Vista turned her thoughts to Doctor Joseph Elam and her appointment the next day. She had only met him once, several years before. The Maestro had taken suddenly ill after his concert with the San Francisco Symphony at the San Francisco Civic Center.

As she watched the neon lights from Kearny Street dance on the ceiling, her thoughts went back to that concert. She fell asleep remembering the strains of the *Warsaw Concerto,* and the Maestro caressing the strings of his three hundred year old *Straivarius.* How handsome the Maestro had looked that night in his white tie and tails. He had a special smile that he only gave to his vast audience. She waited always for the end of the concert and that haunting and charismatic smile.

Vista had such a strong feeling for the past that she could almost realize being there, hearing the music, smell the perfume of the vast audiences and be for the moment with those she loved in that past moment of time. Suppose that sometime she got caught up in the time warp of her mind, never to return to the present. The thought frightened her, yet she knew she would experience an aroma, a sight, a special melody and would again return to her world of yesterday. She was anxious for Dolly's return. She was not used to being alone.

CHAPTER THREE

A Lady Lost

Doctor Morris Elam finished his tests and examination and sat down in his high back leather chair across the desk from Vista. His heavy white brows furrowed over compassionate eyes told Vista what she knew in her heart and dreaded to hear.

"Have you been to another Doctor, Vista?"

"No. I don't want to worry my children."

"You won't be able to keep the fact that you have Alzheimers disease from them. They must have guessed something is wrong, Vista." He was trying to be gentle with her using her first name.

"I bought this phony hearing aid, so when I can't answer their questions, I pretend it's the fault of my hearing aid."

"You are a clever lady. It would be funny if it weren't such a sad incurable disease."

"Can't you do anything for me doctor. Pills, diet, an operation on my head, anything!" Vista pleaded.

"I'm sorry. Our scientists are working on it."

"How will it progress Doctor? How fast? How much time do I have?"

"Every person, every case, is different. In some the progression is much slower than others."

"Should I have come to you sooner? Would that have helped?"

"I don't think so. Do you forget telephone numbers, birthdays and where you parked your car?"

"Yes, Doctor, more and more."

"You shouldn't go out alone. You may become frightened and disoriented. You may get lost. Let me call your daughter to come for you. You can have a cup of coffee and wait right here in my office."

"No, Doctor Elam. My Dolly went down the coast today, to Carmel. Just have your nurse call me a taxi. I'm staying at the Ritz Carlton for a few days."

"I don't know. I feel responsible for you. You really should tell your family, Vista."

"Not yet Doctor. Please, just a little while longer."

"This is a disease you have no control over, Vista. I'm so very sorry."

"It's not your fault, Doctor. Should I see a specialist?"

"Yes, it is always good to have more than one opinion."

"Will it happen all at once? I mean, will I forget who I am or who my children are?"

"Very rarely does it happen suddenly. Maybe if you had some trauma. But I suggest you tell your family and stay close to them, so nothing serious will happen to you. You have children who love you and want you to be happy and comfortable in your senior years. Enjoy them, Vista, and let them do for you."

"That's a drastic reversal of rolls, I am used to doing for them."

"Well, now it's your turn. Accept it and enjoy the time you have left."

As vista stepped into the taxi doctor Elam's words kept ringing in her head. Time . . . enjoy the time . . . tears flowed down her cheeks causing the big burly driver to ask, "Are you okay little lady?"

"Yes, Please take me to Nob Hill to the Ritz Carlton."

"No! No! I changed my mind. Take me to Marshall Fields, I need a new hat." Vista said as she replaced her key for her hotel back in her jacket pocket. A new hat always made her feel better. She looked towards the sky and shook her fist. You left me money, family, friends, if you could just have left me a good mind, my darling. "Oh dear! I know it's not your fault. But it's easier to blame it on the dead. I still love you." she mumbled.

"Are you okay lady? You're talking to yourself." The driver said, his heavy black brows crossing his forehead and his piercing black eyes saying she was a nutty lady.

"Just praying, young man, just praying."

"My driving that bad?"

"You could slow down on the next curve." They both laughed.

"Marshall Fields, Mam. That will be five bucks."

"Keep the change. The extra five is for slowing down on that last turn."

Thank you, Lady! Have a good day and stop crying and praying. Go have a good time."

She would shop, have an early dinner at the hotel and relax and watch TV. Watching TV made her think of Nickoel back in Houston. She would call her when she got back to the hotel. Counting the three hours difference in time, she would just be arriving home from work. She went over Nickoel's telephone number in her mind. 876-9707, 876-9707 . . .

As she stepped from the taxi, she saw two young men sprinting down the side walk towards her. She expected them to pass her and keep running. They did, but not until after they knocked her down and grabbed her purse.

A well groomed man slightly older then Vista helped her to her feet. "Are you hurt Lady?" He asked.

"No. Just my dignity."

"Let me take you home."

"No! Just get me a taxi, please."

As Vista sat in the taxi she couldn't remember where she was going. "Just take me for a ride around the city." She told the oriental driver.

Vista's hand touched the key in her pocket. She pulled it out and read, Ritz Carlton. "Take me to the Ritz Carlton she ordered the taxi."

"Where you get money to pay? I see them take away your purse."

"Why didn't you catch them for me?"

"I no policeman, Lady. I taxi driver."

"Don't worry. I have money." Vista felt in her brazier where she kept her big bills, pinned in a small silk bag. She had often thought of designing a bra with a pocket closed by velcro for the women to hide their big bills in. She laughed to herself. The first time she thought of it was back in the sixties when women were burning their bras, so she gave up on the idea.

Now, she remembered her credit cards in her purse would have to be canceled. She could not remember what cards she had. Grandmother Vista had been right, years before when she said credit was no good. She wondered if she were alive today, what she would think of credit cards.

Vista went to the room number on her key. It wouldn't open the door. She went back to the lobby to engage some help to get her into her room. "What is your name please?" The desk clerk asked. A name? Yes, her name. "Dora Smith." She said, extending her key.

"I'm sorry that key is registered to someone else. Do you have some identification." The pert young blonde behind the desk asked.

"No some fellows knocked me down and stole my purse with my credit cards."

"I'm sorry we can't help you unless you show some I.D . . ."

"But I just showed you the key. My clothes must be in that room."

"I'm sorry the name you just gave does not match the name on our records. We don't know where you got that key."

"I got it this morning when I checked in." Vista could not remember but her daughter Dolly had checked her in while she had coffee in the coffee shop.

"We can give you another room. But if your credit cards were stolen how will you pay?" The blonde's tone of voice was very business like.

"I will pay cash. Vista reached into her bra and pulled out an abundant roll of large bills. Do you want me to pay now or when I check out."

"The clerk must have been impressed at the amount of money Vista had in her hand. "That's fine Mrs. Smith. You may pay when you check out tomorrow. I'm so sorry you lost your purse. Please fill out the register."

"May I take it over there. I want to sit down, I still feel rather shaky." Vista said, pointing to a chair and table in the lobby that looked like it had been retrieved from the *Ming Dynasty.*

"Of course, how thoughtless of me. Take your time. We have a room ready for you."

Dora Smith she put down, but what was her home address and telephone number. She would have to make it all fiction. She could correct it tomorrow when she remembered who she was. She wrote, 353 Boling Way, Chicago Ill. and a fictitious telephone number. She wondered who she really was.

"Please, remember Mrs. Smith the number on the key does not correspond with the room number for security purposes." The clerk warned her.

"Please write it down for me." Vista asked. Then placed the number in her jacket pocket. A bell hop escorted her to her room.

"Enjoy your stay, Mrs. Smith."

As Vista watched the city lights come on, she tried to remember her name. She was hungry and ordered from the room service menu. She stayed in the room for three days ordering her meals from room service and trying hard to remember who she was and if she lived in San Francisco. She guessed not or she wouldn't be staying in a hotel.

On the fourth day she decided to go down to the lobby shops and buy a new purse and maybe a new hat. Did she like hats? She put on her big yellow picture hat and studied herself in the mirror. Maybe she was trying too hard. She took some of the big bills out and put them in the pocket of her yellow silk dress. The rest she put back in her bra and arranged her white silk scarf around her neck.

She bought a new suit and wondered why she was wearing such a flimsy dress. San Francisco was a chilly town, especially after sundown.

She wore the new navy suit and purchased a big brimmed red hat and red silk scarf. She was at the handbag counter trying to decide between a red leather and a navy eel skin purse. A man's voice broke her concentration. "You should take the blue one. You will get more use out of it. It will go with more costumes. I see you got over your ghastly experience the other day. You look lovely." It was the man who had helped her to her feet, and helped her into the taxi.

She remembered! If she remembered that, maybe other things would come back to her soon. She felt light hearted as she purchased the navy eel skin bag. Vista thanked him for his help. Her smile was very beguiling. "You do look lovely." The good looking stranger said. "I have been contemplating lunch. I hate eating alone. Would you join me, please?"

"Yes. That would be nice." Vista liked his engaging smile, his nice manners and his velvety baritone voice.

"I worried about you after you got in the cab. It all happened so fast. I chastised myself for not seeing you to your destination. Are you staying in the hotel?"

"Yes."

"So am I. Oh dear! I could have brought you here. I wish I would have known."

He directed her to a little pub around the square from the hotel. As they were being seated he extended his hand to her, "I am John Farley." He was still holding her hand and asking, "And what is your name, Dear Lady?"

Oh Goodness! she couldn't remember. What would she say?

The television above the bar caught her eye. It was displaying a coffee commercial advertizing the coffee's mild aroma. "Mild Aroma." She said, her eyes meeting his warm concerned brown ones.

"Mild Aroma! That's a strange name."

"No. Milo Aroma."

"Aroma. That must be Italian."

"Oh yes. My late husband's name was Aroma."

"I see. He's deceased?"

"Yes, several years ago."

"I'm sorry."

"What is the cuisine of this restaurant?"

"English, I believe."

"You order for me. You make such wise choices." Vista said referring to her new handbag.

They ate slowly. John Farley delighted in telling her of his escapades in the diplomatic service of his country. She could tell he was a devout American and ever so proud of his country and his job. His next tour of duty would start next week. He was being sent to Israel.

John Farley mistook Milo's reticence for feminine mystique.

"I don't want to let you go. I am enjoying your company so much. Will you join me for a symphony concert tonight? They are playing *Beethoven*, my favorite."

"Mine too." She lied. Who was her favorite composer?. She wished she could remember.

They had seats in the orchestra. John took her hand in his and held it all during the concert. Vista . . . Milo didn't seem to mind. She felt very content with John Farley.

They had a late night supper and John escorted her to her room. He noticed the chocolate on her laid down bed.

"Nice touch. Do have sweet dreams, Dear Lady." He said as he kissed her hand. I am afraid you are stealing my heart away. May I kiss you goodnight?"

Before she could say no or yes she was in his arms. He kissed her tenderly and released her. "I like you too much, Milo Aroma. I'll call you in the morning."

After John left she wrote down his name and the name Milo Aroma. She must not forget.

The next morning they met for breakfast. She needed to buy some more clothes. "I need to go shopping. I didn't bring enough clothes."

"May I go with you?"

"Won't you be bored?"

"Not at all". He hailed a cab and took her to Nieman Marcus. She was worried that she might not have enough money.

"I don't know, this store is expensive and I have lost my credit cards."

"We'll use mine."

"No! No! I couldn't do that."

"Nonsense. You are a lady in distress. You can pay me later."

As the models passed by them, John picked the costumes he liked and the big brimmed hats to match.

"You have excellent taste Monsieur. You look so familiar. Are you a celebrity?" The sales girl asked.

"I don't think so."

"Now, I remember. You are, John Farley, the foreign diplomat. I saw your picture in the Society news."

"You are very well informed Miss."

"It is part of our job to study the Society Columns, so we will know who our patrons are when they come into our salon. That way we can give them extra attention." Then she turned to Milo. "You are so lucky to have such a devoted husband." The sales girl said looking Milo over in a glance of approval.

John and Milo laughed. "You see, Milo, we look like we belong together." John whispered in her ear.

Maybe it was the power of suggestion of the sales girl.

That evening after a whirlwind day of shopping and sipping tea in many quaint little shops, John proposed marriage.

John's eyes sparkled and his cheeks had a rosy glow that was not there a week ago. They had been together constantly all their waking hours. John only returned to his room to sleep. He called her early every morning.

"I'll be down soon. We will have coffee in your room."

John was anxious to hear the answer to his last evening's proposal.

Milo had made the remark that she would have to leave soon as her cash was running out and she had no credit cards.

"It would be much wiser and cheaper if we were married. Then we would only need one suite." John said in a serious manner.

"Are you proposing, John?"

"Yes, of course I am. I'm a little old to get down on one knee, you might have to help me up."

"I'll have to think about it. Maybe, call my family."

"But you said you had no family."

"Not one I know about." She laughed nervously. Did she have a family? "I have a cousin I've always kept in touch with."

"Great, invite her to our wedding."

"I don't think so. She is not well." Vista lied.

Milo wondered if she should tell John that she didn't know who she was. Then she would have to tell him she had an incurable disease. Besides it wasn't a contagious disease. And if she had a family wouldn't they have been with her or found her here at the hotel, she had been here ten days already. She loved John and his colorful stories about the foreign diplomatic service. He was gentle and caring and he needed her too. They were happy together. And she guessed she must be entitled to this last bit of happiness in her life. She just wished she had a family to share her happiness. Maybe when the men knocked her down, she hit her head. Maybe she had a slight concussion, and her memory would eventually come back. It might not be the Alzheimer's at all. Besides, Doctor what's his name?, said it came on gradually. How many days had it been? She would have to ask John.

A telephone number came to mind. Milo went to the phone. John would be down soon. Milo dialed, 9, for an outside line, then 876-9707.

"Johnny's Pizza" a voice came over the phone. "Hello! Hello! We are not open until noon." Milo replaced the phone and wondered why that number came to her. She felt it had something to do with her past.

"Why the long face?" John asked as he came through the door with the room service waiter. "Over there, by the window." He ordered the waiter carrying their breakfast tray. Then he handed him a tip.

"A telephone number keeps going around in my head and I don't know who it belongs to."

"Let me try it." He said picking up the phone. 876-9707.

"Pizza." John said.

"No Pizza! We have string beans, onions and all kinds of fruit, but yes! we'll have no pizza today." John sang and Milo joined in. Imitating an old song popular in the twenties, *Yes! We Have No Bananas Today.*

"You remember that one, John?"

"Yes, I do. And *I'm Forever Blowing Bubbles, and Let Me Call You Sweetheart*."

"My aunt gave me a player piano when I was little for my Birthday. We played those old rolls, *On The Good Ship Lolli Pop*, one of Shirley Temples songs." . . . Milo remembered that, maybe the rest would come back.

"You have a lovely voice Milo."

"I used to sing in the Church choir." Yes, she did. What Choir? . . . Where?

John replaced the phone in its cradle, went to the table and poured their coffee. His back was to her when he asked "Will you marry me, Milo?" He was afraid she might say no, and he didn't want her to see the look of rejection on his face.

"Why not?" Milo said cheerfully.

John set down the silver coffee pot and took Milo in his arms. "I have been so lonely all these years. You have brought me happiness beyond measure. I hope you like to travel."

"Yes, of course. Where are we going?"

"To Israel. My next assignment. Have you ever been to Israel?"

"No. But I have always wanted too." Had she? "You won't leave me in some foreign country will you? I might get lost." Milo continued.

"Never, Milo. We will be together forever." John hugged her close and kissed her gently. Her bath robe fell away revealing her baby blue lace under garments. Milo could feel John's heart beating wildly. "May I have some coffee?" she asked. John released his tight hold on her.

Milo had felt his manliness in that embrace. They had the magic of each other. What else did they need? Soon enough she would remember or would she forget to try to remember? All that mattered at the moment, they had each other. She would stay close to John, as long as she had him she would never be lost again.

They had a simple ceremony at the Town Hall. Judge Barnes was an old acquaintance of John's and had everything ready for them, including the press. John Farley was news worthy, being a Foreign Diplomat. The next day was Sunday and their picture was front page in the San Francisco newspapers.

It was soon common knowledge that the hotels favorite couple had been married. They were moved to the honeymoon suite, compliments of the Ritz Carlton. The concierge sent champaign, a basket of fruit, and two arrangements of exotic flowers to the bridal suite.

Milo wondered if she had ever been this happy and content before.

They left for Israel the next morning. They promised to return to the Ritz, when they returned to the States.

"When we return, I will take you to my, our, mountain top home in Los Angeles, that overlooks the Pacific Ocean. It suits you. Lady of the Mansion. My Milo." He lifted the broad brim of her red hat and kissed her there on the sidewalk in front of all the well-wishers from the Ritz. They applauded as Milo and John Farley entered the taxi to go to the airport and their destination, Israel.

CHAPTER FOUR

Alone Again

The new Mrs. John Farley loved Haifa, Israel. There was so much to see, so much to comprehend. Haifa rises above the Mediterranean on three levels. They were having coffee at a sidewalk café in Hadar Carmel, the middle Haifa. The pink table clothes wafted gently in the soft breeze. Below them was the Old City and the port. Above them was the 1,728-foot Mt. Carmel, extolled in the *Song Of Solomon* for it's beauty. Today John had promised to take Milo up the slopes of the grand mountain to visit the ancient Carmelite Monastery, dating back to the crusaders era.

"Tomorrow, we will take the shore excursion to the lands where the people of the Bible trod." John said as he reached across the table and took her hand in his. The thought of standing in the places where Jesus had given his famous sermons, caused a thrill of excitement to run up Milo's spine. What had she done to deserve such a marvelous man as John Farley. She raised his hand to her lips. "Why Mrs. Farley." John exclaimed.

"God must have sent you to pick me up that day on the side walk in San Francisco. I do love you John. No matter what the future holds, don't ever forget these last two weeks."

Would she still remember these two weeks if she got back her memory?

"Are you feeling well, Milo?. We don't have to go up the mountain today."

"I'm fine John."

"I saw you take a couple aspirins yesterday. You hit your head pretty hard when you were knocked down that day in San Francisco. I notice you don't take any other prescription drugs. I don't either. We're lucky. You are not one to complain, I've noticed. You will tell me if anything is bothering you, Milo?"

"Yes, of course. I just had a small headache. I think it was just the long flight. You never told me how you got our passports so fast." Milo said changing the subject. She hated discussing illnesses.

"That wasn't difficult. I'm a government diplomat so that gives me access to people in the right places."

The waiter approached and John spoke to him in French. Milo loved hearing him speak all the languages in his soothing baritone voice. That morning he had haggled with a merchant in the Old City, in Arabic. The merchant handed over a handsome gold necklace which John placed around her neck. The deal must have gone well for the old Arab, for he smiled a broad toothless smile and bowed to her. She felt he must be laughing at John behind the wide sleeves of his dirty jubbah.

It was midmorning, a week after they arrived in Haifa. They sipped coffee at their favorite sidewalk café' overlooking the port and the blue Mediterranean. A young man with piercing black eyes, dressed in a grey business suit and wearing a white kaffiyeh, headdress, delivered a note to John and left quickly.

John read the note and looked about him furtively. He asked Milo to please walk alone to the nearest street corner, he would meet her there. Milo had not finished her breakfast.

"Go quickly. Do as I say. Please! Milo."

"What's wrong John?"

"Go! Please." John's voice was strained and tainted with something like fear. Milo followed his directions. He caught up with her. He escorted her down an alley way and into the back door of the hotel. They took their bags and slipped out the back way, without bothering to check out. They changed to three taxi's before they settled into a small out of the way hotel.

"Milo started to unpack. "No! Keep everything packed. We will be leaving first thing tomorrow. I have been reassigned." John said his voice still sounding strange.

"Where, John?"

"I'm not sure. Another messenger will contact me to-morrow. I should not have brought you here. There is too much unrest in this country. When I get back tomorrow, I will send you home and follow as soon as I can. I love you too much to put you in danger."

That night as they lay entwined in an embrace, she felt the tenseness of his body, like he was expecting something to happen. The next morning John left, telling Milo to stay in the hotel room until he returned.

The hours stretched into three days. John never returned.

Milo was hungry. The room service was very bad. She was afraid to leave, afraid John would return and find her gone. She knew he was in trouble. She did not want to add to his burden.

Finally on the third day, she went to the shabby lobby and asked the desk clerk if there was a message for her. There was none. She felt so alone.

Milo decided to go to the sidewalk cafes' they had frequented. She wore her navy suit and wide brimmed hat with her large sunglasses. A warm breeze billowed the tablecloths of the sidewalk cafe' as she passed.

Such a beautiful day. Nothing bad could happen on a day like this. John would return to her soon. Milo became more alarmed as the hours passed. She saw a beautiful music box in a shop window. She wanted to buy it for her granddaughter. The little dancing ballerina on top reminded her of Nickoel. Yes! She had a granddaughter. She remembered. Milo purchased the little box and gave the shop owner the address in the United States, to mail it to her. Milo slipped a note inside the box. 'I will see you soon. I love you. Always, Grandmother'.

Milo carefully put her granddaughters address in her billfold. She could hardly wait to tell John that she had a granddaughter. She was so excited that she walked several blocks before she remembered that she had left her purse in the shop.

When she returned to the shop another Arab shop keeper was there. She could not make him understand that she had lost her purse. Milo thought of calling the police, but if John was in some kind of trouble that would not be wise.

She returned to the hotel hoping John would be there. In the excitement of losing her purse she forgot again about Nickoel.

She remembered, John had placed their airline tickets under a drawer in the dilapidated desk along with her passport. When she pulled out the drawer a note fell to the floor.

"Milo, if I am not back within twenty four hours, leave immediately for our home in Los Angeles. Go my darling, I love you. I will meet you in Los Angeles. Don't forget your passport." The note read.

For some reason Milo thought she should leave by the back door. Her credit cards had all been stolen or lost and she might need the money she had hidden in her bosom. She felt she should be as inconspicuous as possible. She hailed a taxi and left for the Haifa airport.

After her long trip she checked in the Waldorf Hotel in New York. She did not sleep well. She was remembering John. She missed sleeping in the curve of his strong arm.

She went to the bedside phone and dialed the number that was always on her mind. 876-9707.

"Hello!" A gruff voice answered.

"Hello. This is Milo Aroma. Do you know me?"

"Hell, no lady. We don't know anyone by that name. You got a wrong number." Milo sat down on the bed. She knew that number belonged to someone in her past.

The next morning she boarded the plane at La Guardia and headed for Los Angeles. Milo had a layover in Houston, Texas. She passed the two hours watching the people mill about.

Tomorrow she would be in Los Angeles. She would find John's Mansion on the mountain and wait for him. She spotted a row of telephones and the telephone number came to her again.

876-9707. She dialed.

This time she got an answering service. The sweet young voice sounded familiar. "This is Milo Aroma." She forgot to use her married name Farley. "I'm sorry you're not at home. I will call again sometime. Have a happy day." She knew that voice. Who was that young girl? She would try again before she boarded the plane. But then, Vista forgot to remember.

CHAPTER FIVE

Search For A Missing Grandmother

"Steve, I tell you something terrible has happened to mother. I told her not to wear her diamonds shopping. We just discussed it last month, when they were having the trouble with the Rolex watch thieves. She only pooh-poohed me. You know how independent she is." James said. "We never should have let her go alone to San Francisco. Especially since we know how irresponsible Dolly can be. She should have gone shopping with her. At her age anything could have happened. It has been almost a month. She is dead. I know it. She's dead." Steve said in a low sad voice.

"Stop it!" Nickoel ordered as she entered the kitchen where the family was having their Saturday morning coffee. "Grandmother is missing, but she is not dead."

Everyone turned to see the angry look on Nickoel's face. The big tears rolled down her cheeks. Her mother came over and put her arm around Nickoel. "You're right dear. Grandmother is just lost. At her age she could have fallen and hit her head and became disoriented."

"If she would have waited a week, I could have gone with her." Nickoel put her head on the table and cried.

"She has been acting strange every since she got that hearing aid." James said. "I hope we didn't make her feel bad. Maybe we shouldn't tease her so much. We forget she is older and probably more sensitive."

"Nonsense. Grandmother Vista has always been a good sport. No, something else has been bothering her." Steve added. "Have you called the San Francisco police this week, George?"

"Yes, Mother. Yesterday I called them and Dolly. Still nothing. Dolly is in tears every time I call. She feels everyone is blaming her, since she was the last one of us to see Mother."

Nickoel brushed her long blonde hair back as she poured her coffee cream with the other hand. "I'm sure she is lost. I spent a lot more time with her than any of you. Steve do you remember when she left her car at the Galleria? You picked it up the next day and nothing was wrong with it. I think she said it wouldn't start to cover up the fact that she could not remember where she had parked the car. She forgot many times what day it was." Nickoel said, as she remembered grandmother's 'What happened to Monday', and how they had laughed. Then she remembered her grandmother Vista quoting a poem, and the corners of her mouth curled as she remembered the words of a poem, her grandmother had quoted that evening.

> Just a line to say I'm living
> That I'm not among the dead;
> 'Tho I'm getting more forgetful
> And mixed up in my head.

"Please grandmother send me that line so I will know you are okay. Please God take care of my grandmother Vista." Nickoel prayed as she headed for her grandmother's room. She sat cross legged in the middle of Vista's bed and thought about the rest of the poem.

> For sometimes, I can't remember
> When I stand upon the stair,
> If I'm going up for something
> Or have just come down from there?
> And before the "fridge" so often,
> My poor mind is filled with doubt,
> Have I just put the food away or
> Have I come to take some out?
> Then there's the time it's dark out
> and my nightcap's on my head.
> I don't know if I'm retiring
> or getting out of bed?

Nickoel smiled through her tears remembering her grandmother's recitation. She buried her head in grandmother's pillow and cried for her lost grandmother, Vista.

The entire family was gathered around the kitchen table "We all forget our cars and what day it is." George said. "That's nothing to get excited about." They sat around blaming each other and consoling each other in turn, about Vista's disappearance.

The doorbell rang. It was Nathan Golden, Nickoel's fiancee'. There had been much ado about the engagement. Nathan was Jewish and Nickoel was Catholic. Nathan's reticent promise that the future children would be raised Catholic, bothered the family.

Nathan was a personable fellow, handsome with dark features and laughing brown eyes. He already had laugh lines around his eyes and mouth. His usual cheerfulness alleviated the families spirits for a little while. "I believe like Nickoel. Mother Vista is alive and we will find her. I'm sure of it. I have to go to San Francisco in a few days for my company. I will see if I can find her." Nathan said with confidence.Esther served them French toast. They all ate in silence, each in their own way missing the heart of the family, Mother Vista.

"Have you set the date, Nathan?" George asked.

"We think we should wait until we find, Mother Vista." Nathan said, his heavy eyebrows knitting across his high forehead. A seldom seen sad expression filled his eyes. George guessed that Nickoel and Nathan had argued on the matter. Nathan stole a glance at Nickoel and saw tears on the cheeks of her bowed head. He found her hand under the table and squeezed it.

"I'm going to San Francisco with you." Nickoel tossed her blonde hair back in a determined fashion.

"I don't think so. That's not wise. You know nothing of the town. We don't want to lose you too." Her mother said. "And what about your work?"

"My work is not as important as my grandmother Vista. Besides, I do have vacation time coming. I will not be alone. I will be with Nathan." Nickoel said emphatically. Nickoel was small of stature but big on determination. "I will call you every night to report on what's happening." She added.

Two days later Nickoel was in San Francisco questioning detective De Sabito on the procedures of finding a missing person. "I have been all through this with your aunt Dolly." His long skinny nose and hawk eyes that seemed to be irritated with her did not match the sympathetic tone in his voice. "We have been working very hard to find your grandmother, Miss. There is only so much we can do. We show pictures around the hospitals, hotels and police stations. We even put a picture in the newspapers." Detective De Sabito said.

"Let me see what picture you have?" Nickoel asked.It was a picture taken in evening attire at some forgotten party, years before. "No one would recognize her from that. She always wears glasses and big hats."

"That was the only one I could find. I'm sorry." Dolly said.

"I brought more recent one's." Nickoel said as she shared the pictures with the Sergeant.

Dolly told Nickoel of the misunderstanding they had the day they went to see Bob Hope. "I thought she was still angry with me and that was why she insisted on going shopping alone."

Nickoel had never knew her grandmother to stay angry for more then five minutes. Grandmother Vista said it was a waste of good time, that would be better spent in some positive attitude. "I think grandmother is lost. I think she has forgotten who she is. She has been getting very forgetful lately. She pretends to be hard of hearing but I know better.

Grandmother and I have always been very close. Don't worry Aunt Dolly, we will find her. It's not your fault. I know and so does everyone else how independent she can be." She hugged her Aunt Dolly. Tomorrow she would take the pictures to the Ritz Carlton.

The next morning Nickoel and Dolly went early to the yellow cab co. They were lucky the shifts were changing so they could question more drivers. One driver who was in a hurry to get to his little girls birthday party, recognized the picture of Vista in her picture hat and oversized sunglasses. "She was a nice lady. I took her to a doctor's office on Van Ness."

"Where on Van Ness?" Dolly insisted.

"I told you lady, I have a birthday party to go to."

"Please this is a matter of life and death. The lady you took to the doctor's office that day is still missing. Please! A gift for your little girl." Nickoel placed a twenty dollar bill in the cab drivers hand.

"Sure ladies, I'll check my log book."

"670 Van Ness. I don't know which doctor though."

It was their first lead and they were very excited as they found another driver to take them to Van Ness Street.

"Aunt Dolly, it was the picture of Grandmother in those picture hats that she wears so well. Everyone remembers her. She is a striking lady you know." Nickoel said. Admiration colored her speech.

"And she loves and admires you too, Nickoel. You have made these last few years so pleasant for her, just being there for her."

"We've got to hurry and find her. She needs us Aunt Dolly."

They found Doctor Elam's office. They had to wait a couple hours for the doctor to return from his rounds at the hospital. Nickoel's body tingled with anticipation. Doctor Morris Elam was older then Nickoel had expected. He had a big head and a full shock of silver grey unruly hair that fell over his forehead and met with his thick white eyebrows that knitted in a frown. His fading blue eyes questioned her. "You say you are Vista's daughter and granddaughter. How is she?"

"Doctor she has been missing for several weeks. What is wrong with my grandmother?" Her tension gave way to tears.

"She is in an advanced stage of Alzheimer's disease."

"I knew it! I knew it! She's not dead, just missing."

"She seemed rational when she left here. That was more than a month ago. We called a cab for her. She was staying at the Ritz

Carlton. I wanted her to call her daughter, but she insisted on calling a taxi." The doctor said a worried look on his weathered face.

"Is there any hope for a cure for her, Doctor?"

"No. There is no cure for Alzheimer's disease. All you can do is keep her comfortable and as happy as possible."

"How much time does Mother have?" Dolly asked.

"Maybe a couple more years. You must feel free to call me any time you have questions."

Nickoel showed the picture of her grandmother to the receptionist and asked her what taxi she had called for her.

She checked her appointment book for the last month and told them that she had called the Yellow Taxi and it was around one o'clock. "I remember she was wearing s summer dress and the weather had turned chilly that day. I thought she needed a sweater." The middle aged receptionist said. "She had just came here from Houston and the temperature there was quite hot."

Now Nickoel had to worry about her grandmother being dressed warm. She had helped her pack and she had only brought summer clothes.

The taxi's shifts changed around three. She would have to wait until the next day.

"That night Nickoel lay in Nathan's arms crying. "Nathan, she is alive. Grandmother Vista is alive and she needs me."

"You don't know for sure Nicky. She has been gone for over a month." The look of concern on his tanned face was partly for himself. All of Nickoel's attentions were directed to the finding of grandmother Vista. He felt some what slighted. He was unhappy that Nickoel had postponed their wedding. If she truly loved him, shouldn't he come first? Then he felt guilty, for he loved the old lady too. He would do everything he could to help Nickoel find her.

"I would know if anything bad had happened to grandmother. We are very close." Nathan could not argue with her logic.

"You are a great detective, Honey."

"It was the picture. Everyone remembers an attractive lady who wears big hats, no matter what her age. I'm so glad I insisted on coming." Nathan Golden held her close and knew that if he ever needed a friend he could count on Nickoel.

Nickoel found the taxi driver who had taken Vista to Marshall Fields department store. There the trail ended. It was as though, her grandmother had dropped off the face of the earth. She stood for hours in front of the department store showing grandmother Vista's picture to everyone. She went to all the hotels and restaurants in the area around Nob Hill.

The Ritz Carlton said she had only stayed one day. That her clothes had been left in the room. They gave her Vista's luggage. Knowing that her grandmother did not have her clothes frightened Nickoel. Maybe she had been kidnapped.

Nathan had to return home and he insisted Nickoel come along. There was nothing more she could do. She would have to leave it to the police.

Nickoel played back the week's messages on her phone recorder. Near the end of the tape came a familiar voice. "Hello! This is Milo Aroma. I'm sorry you're not at home. Do have a happy day. I will call again sometime." That was her grandmother. She always used that expression 'Have a happy day'. But why was she calling herself, Milo Aroma. She called the family in and they listened to it over and over and they all agreed it was grandmother Vista.

"I'm going back to San Francisco." Nickoel announced. "And I am staying until I find her."

"How about your job. They will fire you and you like your job." her mother argued. She was legal secretary for a prominent law firm.

"There are other jobs. There is only one Grandmother Vista. Uncle Steve will you get me a flight right away?"

"Today? Don't you want to wait a day or so. You just got back from San Francisco. Nathan will not like you going alone." Steve countered.

"No! I want to leave as soon as possible. Hurry! Uncle Steve." Steve looked at his mother. She looked unhappy but Esther knew nothing she could do or say would change Nickoel's determination to find her grandmother. She nodded her head in silent consent.

Nickoel took more pictures of Vista this time. The best she could find. Now she had a name, Milo Aroma. Was Milo Aroma really her grandmother Vista?

Nickoel's evenings were lonely without Nathan. Dolly had her own circle of friends. She always invited her niece but Nickoel was too tired and too unhappy to be good company to anyone. "You know aunt Dolly, Grandmother liked nice places. Tomorrow I'm going back to Nob Hill to all the hotels again." And Nickoel wondered as she looked around Aunt Dolly's 'avant garde' apartment, what her grandmother thought of it. Then she remembered her grandmother was very adaptable and she hoped that quality in her would keep her alive until she could find her and take her home.

"I'll go with you tomorrow." Aunt Dolly said.

"That's not necessary. I will keep you posted on my progress." Nickoel knew Dolly was anxious to finish the mural she was painting for the Top Of The Mark.

Nickoel took a poster board and pasted several pictures of Grandmother Vista in place. She would try the new Ritz Carlton again tomorrow.

"Yes. She looks very familiar, but we see so many people." The reserved young girl behind the desk said. "I'm sorry we can't help you."

Nickoel started to walk away and turned back to the desk. "Please try the name, Milo Aroma. It would have been about a month ago."

The young Oriental girl went to the computer and pulled up August. "Yes, we had a, Milo Aroma. She stayed almost three weeks."

"Please check the phone calls from her room."

"I had better talk to my manager. I don't know if I should be giving you this information."

"Look lady! my Grandmother has Alzheimers and she has been missing for over a month. If you want me to call the Police Lieutenant who is working on this case I will. I only want to know what calls she made from her room."

"Just one outside call, 876-9707."

"What area code?"

"None. Just 876-9707.

A tall girl still adjusting her tie had just come on duty and spotted the pictures of Vista. That's the lady who wore the big hats. I especially liked the red one. She was an elegant dresser."

"You remember her?"

"Oh yes! She was very charming. We were all invited to her little wedding reception here at the hotel. We felt sorry that neither of them had any relatives. They were a darling couple."

"Wedding!"

"Oh yes. She married a handsome older man. He stays here often. He is some kind of foreign diplomat."

"He is a foreigner?"

"No. He is an American who is a foreign diplomat." She smoothed the back of her up swept hairdo. "Who are you?"

"I am her granddaughter."

"But we understood she had no relatives."

"That's because my grandmother has Alzheimer and sometimes forgets us."

"What was the man's name?" Nickoel asked unable to hide the excitement in her voice.

"Oh dear, I don't remember."

"It wasn't Aroma?"

"No. That was the name she went by. They made a handsome couple. He adored her. They were always shopping. He bought her beautiful jewels and clothes. Oh yes! They were leaving for some country abroad. That's all I remember."

"Please try to remember. Please! Help me. She is my grandmother." Nickoel began to sob uncontrollably.

"Please Miss. Sit over here." Brian Price the manager had been summoned. He had his arm around Nickoel and was escorting her to an Oriental chair in the lobby. "Don't cry, Miss . . . Bard! bring the lady a glass of water." The Manager ordered the bellman. "We will help you."

"She is my grandmother and we thought she was dead. Please help me. Maybe someone else remembers her . . . I mean them."

The staff turns over pretty fast in a new hotel. Let me think who would have been here a month ago. Alma. Alma Young. But she works nights."

"I'll come back around four o'clock. Thank you, Mr . . . ?"

"Price. I hope you locate your grandmother."

"Thank you Mr. Price."

'She's not lost, just relocated and remarried and hard to tell what else'. Nickoel thought as she went out the front and entered the cab, the doorman had waiting for her. "Kearny Street." She told the driver. She took another tissue from her purse and began to cry softly. Her grandmother had a new love in her life, maybe she wouldn't need her anymore. She felt a heaviness around her heart. She decided not to tell Aunt Dolly until she found out tomorrow if it was her grandmother who married the foreign diplomat. It was unbelievable that this could be happening. Her cookie baking grandmother, married to some stranger!

Was she being kept against her will? Did the man kidnap her and take her out of the country. All kinds of strange ideas came to Nickoel's mind. The people at the hotel said they were such a nice couple. She ate lunch without any awareness of what she was eating, a sense of loss churning her stomach.

Late that afternoon, Nickoel was waiting for Alma Young. "Oh Yes. She was an unforgettable lady. She was such fun. She loved life and people. We all watched them and wished they belonged to our family. She was in the hotel for almost a month. She wore beautiful clothes and big hats and fancy big sun glasses. She married a foreign diplomat. They made such a handsome couple. Mr. Farley really loved her. We used to watch him when he stayed here before. He never got close to any of the lady guests. He always seemed so alone. He was so charming we couldn't understand why he never had a woman companion before. There are always society widows staying here in the hotel."

"You say his name was, Farley?"

"I ought to know. I was in charge of getting the napkins and matches printed for the wedding reception. I still have some in my locker. It was the first wedding here at the new Ritz Carlton and the staff was pretty excited about it, especially since we admired them so much."

Alma said pausing for breath. "Who are you?"

"I am her granddaughter, Nickoel." She said offering her trembling hand to Alma.

"But we understood she didn't have any relatives." Don't cry honey." Alma said patting Nickoel's hand.

"She has Alzheimer. We didn't know it until after she was lost. She has been gone for more then a month."

"Oh Dear! She seemed perfectly normal to all of us. Are you sure? Maybe it's not the same woman." Nickoel pulled Vista's picture from her purse.

"Yes, that's her. If you wait I will go and get the matches and the newspaper. They had their pictures on the front page. They were married by one of Mr. Farley's friends Judge Joseph Finkel. Don't cry honey, they were very happy."

"What country?"

"I don't remember. But wherever it was, they were going to honeymoon there."

"Did they leave a forwarding address? How about his home address?. Will you get them for me?"

"Sure Miss . . ."

"Nickoel Conrad." She answered.

Alma returned." All I could find was a Washington address and phone number. Goodbye, Miss Conrad. I hope you find your grandmother soon."

Nickoel looked again at the handsome couple in the newspaper Alma had given her. Grandmotrher Vista looked happy. Why did the picture wrench at her heart? She resented not being a part of her grandmothers life. What had happened?

Nickoel rushed to the telephone, her heart beating wildly. She felt she was very close to finding grandmother Vista. She dialed the number and got the diplomatic service in Washington. She was told that they could not give out information on anyone. These were desperate times. "But he married my grandmother. She's very ill and I must find her. Mr. Farley doesn't know about her illness." Nickoel explained.

"Sorry miss. I can only tell you his dossier states that he is a widower. That's all I can tell you." The phone clicked, sounding like the end of the world to the devastated Nickoel. She had to find someone with important friends in Washington. She went back to Dolly's apartment on Kearny and cried herself to sleep. Her only solace was that grandmother had a good man taking care of her by all accounts.

The next day she went to the court house to talk to Judge Finkel. "I'm sorry, Miss Conrad, I can't tell you more. I was more surprised than any one that my old friend was marrying.

John Farley has been a widower for twelve years. He didn't tell me where his new assignment was taking him and his new bride." Nickoel was sure he knew more than he was telling her.

After Nickoel filled Aunt Dolly in on all she had learned she returned to Houston. Every night she listened intently to the days calls as they played back. None from grandmother Vista re. Grandmother Milo re. Mrs. Farley. They had been so extremely close. Surely she had forgotten Nickoel or she would have called.

That night, lightning streaked the sky and the thunder resounded through the villa. Nickoel crept down to grandmother's bed. Tonight she was more afraid for her grandmother than she was of the raging storm. The empty bed held little comfort for her. As the lightening lit up the room, Nickoel remembered grandmother saying *God was in his Heaven and all was right with the World.* Well it wasn't right. Grandmother was out there in the big world alone. "Please God take care of her" Nickoel prayed.

"If your grandmother is married then why can't we set the date?" Nathan complained.

"Not yet. Not until we find grandmother. Do you know anyone who knows anyone in Washington?"

"My uncle knows Senator John Glen of Ohio."

"You never told me that before."

"You never asked."

"You will call your uncle right now?" And she handed Nathan the phone. His uncle promised to call him the next day.

Nathan called the next morning. "It is not spelled out for certain it's difficult to get that information. It is believed that he was sent to Haifa, Israel. And, he did recently marry."

"Did you get an address and telephone number?" Nickoel demanded.

"No. Of course not. They are not allowed to give out that information. We are lucky we got that much. There is much trouble in those countries."

"If it's that dangerous, why did he take grandmother to such a place."

"I am going to Israel." Nickoel said emphatically.

"No! You are not going." The family all spoke at once.

"If she is married then she has someone taking care of her." Her mother said. "Your grandmother has always been very adept at taking care of herself." Esther continued.

"Mother! Your mother has Alzheimer disease. You don't seem to understand that she doesn't even know her own name.

And her new husband doesn't know she is ill." Nickoel broke into tears and ran from the room. Her mother looked perplex-ed and helpless. I know there is no stopping her and there is so much trouble in those countries now. And a young woman alone." Mother Conrad began to cry as well.

"We are a house divided." Mr. Conrad said and he went to his workshop in the garage. He hated any kind of discontent. He was a good provider and worked hard to keep the family on an even keel. He was one of those rare individuals who could not understand why everyone was not happy.

"Can't you go with her Nathan?" Esther pleaded.

"If she will just give me a few days to reorganize my schedule."

As Nickoel came into the dining room she said, "I am not going to wait for you."

"Yes you are, and you stop being so impetuous." Nathan said with a new found sternness.

"You're not married to me yet and even if you were you couldn't tell me what to do." But Nickoel waited. She scanned the World News to see if she could find out anything about Israel. Desert Storm, had just ended. Grandmother Vista was in the midst of all that turmoil. Nickoel was watching the evening news and consuming a chocolate fudge sundae as she sat in the middle of grandmother's bed. She heard the name Farley and spilled her ice cream sundae rushing to find the volume control.

'*Diplomat John Farley was found shot to death, in a back street, yesterday in the Old Port City of Haifa, Israel. His new bride is missing. It is believed that he was carrying important government documents.*'

Nickoel went crazy screaming at everyone. Her father came in from the garage and tried to calm her. She called

Nathan and told him what had happened and that she was leaving at once.

"But you don't have a passport?"

"Yes, I do. I got it before I left San Francisco."

"Please! Baby, Don't go until I am ready." Nathan begged.

No one could stop her. She left the next morning before anyone was awake. The Villa was silent as she left to take the taxi to Houston's Hobby Airport.

She had a lay over at New York's La Guardia Airport. She went to an airport bar to watch the TV news. Her grandmother was still missing.

Nickoel spent a week showing the picture of her grandmother to shop keepers in Haifa. Was she dead too? Maybe they had not found her body yet. Where was she?

On a Friday afternoon Nickoel called her Mother. She told her that a gift from her grandmother had arrived from Haifa, a music box with a dancing ballerina.

Esther checked the date it had been sent and the shop where it had been purchased. The date was four days after the death of John Farley. Nickoel decided she should take the newspaper clipping to show to the shop keeper.

It seemed to be a pleasant shop. The shop keeper smiled and Nickoel wondered if he understood English. He did and she brought the newspaper clipping from her purse. The man studied it and told her he would be back and that she should wait. He was gone for some fifteen minutes when two men in Arab dress entered the shop. They walked over to her, one on each side. They lifted her off her feet causing her to drop her purse. They were laughing at how small she was and did not notice the purse. At least it seemed that way to Nickoel. "I want to go to the American Embassy." she said.

"Ah Ha. American Embassy." His voice sounded gravely and they could not stop their idiotic laughing.

"This is not funny fellows. I am an American."

"Ah Ha, she is American." And they laughed some more. They tied a bandage around her eyes. It smelled sweet-sour and rancid. Probably hashish, Nickoel told herself.

It seemed they traveled for a long time. The car was roomy, probably a limousine. She could feel the car going up what seemed like hills. She tried to remember the outside sounds from the open window. Once she heard church bells. She heard the bleating of sheep and felt the car slow down letting whatever was bleating, time to pass. She could smell fresh mown hay or grass and knew they were riding along country roads.

When they stopped and took her out, they removed the cloth from her eyes. The view was breathtaking. Below her were acres and acres of vineyards and beyond was the blue Mediterranean. The sun was setting. A warm golden sunset merged with the sea. The men grabbed her arms roughly and she screamed at them. She was more upset at them for obscuring her view than she was hurt.

A thunderous voice called out from behind her. Nickoel turned to see a handsome man in riding clothes, his black boots were slightly apart in a stance that told Nickoel that he meant business. "Bring her here." he bellowed.

The men half carried and half dragged her fighting all the way up the fifty some steps to the portico of the hillside mansion. "She's a fiery wench boss. And she's got lots of guts. Ain't afraid of nothing."

"You stupid bully. You're not an Arab. Who are you and what do you want with me? I'm here on private business and I demand to see the American Embassy."

"In good time Miss Conrad. First we need to talk." The man in the riding habit said. "Go to the wine cellar and bring us a bottle of Chardane'. We might as well be sociable about this."

"You are an American" Nickoel asked.

"Close. I am a French Canadian. Your friend John Farley was carrying an important dossier. We want it before it falls into the wrong hands." His eyes were black and piercing and his voice was hard and cold as ice.

"I have no knowledge of things like that. I never met the man. He was married to my grandmother. I came to find her."

"We are looking for her also. When was the last time you talked with your grandmother?"

"It has been two months ago. Once she called on my answering service but I wasn't home. What do you want her for?"

"We believe she has the dossier."

"Oh no! How many factions are after Mr.Farley's papers? Grandmother is in great danger?"

"Yes. We need to find her at once."

"Who are you and what do those papers mean to you?" Nickoel asked.

"The less you know the better, for all of us."

"Did you kill grandmother's new husband?"

"No. We only want the dossier."

"I don't have it. May I go now?"

"Why the big rush? You will join me for dinner."

"I don't want to have dinner with you."

"Take Miss Conrad to the guest quarters." The man named Max said. The two men took her arms as before and on the way, two Arab women joined the group. She was escorted around the swimming pool to a guest house lavishly furnished in ebony furniture with inlaid mother of pearl and ornate carvings. Brass lamps of Arabic persuasion lit the room. The oriental carpet gave the room a soft glow. It was difficult for Nickoel to be frightened in such warm surroundings. The two women busied themselves drawing a bath for her. The essence of oils filled her nostrils with the aromatic perfume of spices and flowers. They started to take off her clothes. "I'll do it myself." she said as she undressed and got into the bath. The women had laid out a white silk sari trimmed in gold braid. Nickoel swept her hair up on top of her head, making her look much older. The women sprayed her with perfume and clapped their hands in appreciation. Nickoel felt she was going on stage. Perhaps this was the most important act of her life. She had better play it well, for tomorrow she could be dead. No one, absolutely no one, knew her whereabouts. She shuddered and realized she could disappear just like her poor grandmother.

The women led her back around the pool and into the main house. There was no use running, the guards were probably close by.

The women disappeared, as though the walls had swallowed them up. She stood there in the middle of an atrium waiting to see what would happen next. There was a huge fountain spewing water in the middle and exotic flowers, crimson and salmon colored, climbing up the walls and spilling over the walk ways. And somewhere in the distance she could hear the music of Beethoven. Nickoel sat down on a marble bench and waited. The aroma of spicy food made her realize that she was hungry.

The man Max came from the far door and strode towards her in a confident military stride. "How long are you going to keep me here, Mr . . . ?"

"Max will be sufficient. We will keep you as long as it takes to make sure you don't have what we are looking for."

"Well I don't have it so I will be leaving now. Call your men to take me back to my hotel."

"Aren't you a little bit afraid?"

"No, I am getting pretty hungry and when I get hungry I can get pretty mean."

"You sure are a gutsy little one."

"I'm not little. I just had a birthday. I am twenty two."

"Well, you will live to be much older so meanwhile, let's have dinner." He took her by the elbow and gently ushered her into a huge dining room. Four candelabra each sporting a half dozen candles lit the big hall. Huge paintings of arab horses, men with daggers and Arab dancing girls, lined the walls.

Nickoel did not remember much of the evening only the headiness of the wine and the thrust of Max's black eyes as he watched her every move. Two gold coins hung around his neck and nestled in the thick black hair of his chest. The white silk of his shirt highlighted the bronze color of his skin. He did not look like a man who would harm her or her grandmother.

Next morning Nickoel awoke to the sound of a trickling brook and birds singing. Her head felt heavy. She would never be a great admirer of the God, Bacchus. When she went out into the morning sunlight, she found the trickling brook to be an irrigation system for the olive groves. The mansion seemed to be deserted. Maybe she could run away. She went to the front of the house and looked out over the Mediterranean. Which way would take her back to Haifa?

"Don't even think about it." came Max's baritone voice. It grated on her nerves more than ever this morning and made her want to fight. "You would get lost and get raped and murdered by the mountain bandits." He was doing a good job of frightening her.

"They would have to catch me first. You had better get me back. My fiance will be looking for me." That was not a true statement. Nathan was so angry at her leaving without him that he may never speak to her again.

"Come, breakfast is served."

"I don't want any."

"Come little one. I have a surprise for you."

"Stop calling me that. My name is Nickoel."

They entered a sunny breakfast room just off the atrium. Another man set at the table his head slumped and his back to her. Here is someone I'd like you to meet. The stranger turned to look. "Nickoel!"

"Nathan!"

"I thought you were dead. They wouldn't tell me anything about you. Only that you had been abducted from the streets of Haifa."

They kissed and clung to each other and promised never to let each other go away alone. "Did you find grandmother Vista?"

No. These people are looking for her too. Something about some important papers that her new husband was carrying."

"We had to take you both off the streets. There are too many other spys looking for you. They are not so good as us. They would kill you for nothing and leave your bodies in the desert for the buzzards. You must both get on the airplane today and out of the country, back to your United States. This is no place for you to be. Mrs. Farley has gone back to the United States. My men followed her to Los Angeles. They lost her there several weeks ago."

"Nathan! Grandmother is alive."

They did not talk much on the plane. They just held hands, thankful to be together again. "Nathan, why did that Max fellow let us go?"

"He didn't. Check the man in the grey suit and fez in the back of the plane. If he gets off in Amsterdam or London I'm wrong. It's my guess, we are the chicks leading the fox to the old hen, Grandmother Vista."

CHAPTER SIX

Vista Is Kidnapped

The morning sun warmed Milo as she walked down Ventura Boulevard in Los Angeles. The big rim of her red hat bounced jauntily as she walked. She wore a navy dress with gold buttons and red accessories. The way she carried herself made her appear to be a lady of importance.

The pink table clothes waving gently in the ocean breeze made Milo think of John and their honeymoon in Haifa, Israel. She hoped he would come soon. She would wait at the hotel for another day. She did not relish going to a big house in the mountains alone. She took a sunlit corner table. She wondered why older people were always cold and tried to remember her age. John had asked her. When she hesitated he laughed and said, "You women either don't tell your age or you fudge."

Milo just couldn't remember. There were a lot of things she could not remember. Oh well! She was not going to spoil this beautiful day. She intended to enjoy herself.

John would join her soon and she would become Lady of his Mansion. She wondered what it would be like. She decided she would leave after breakfast. She would call a taxi and go to the address John had given her.

She was still thinking of John when a pleasant voice asked. "May I join you?"

"Of course." It would never occur to Milo to wonder why a strange young girl would want to join her, when there were so many vacant tables at the sidewalk cafe'.

"I just had to come over and tell you how much I admire your hat, your whole ensemble. You look lovely." The young girl said. Her auburn hair was shinning in the morning sun. She had warm brown eyes and a winning smile.

"Well, thank you Miss."

"Bring me coffee and a doughnut." She ordered the waiter. She had a brash way about her.

"Are you staying around here?"

"Yes. Up the street at the Hilton." Milo said watching the girl's auburn hair ruffle in the breeze. She reminded Milo of someone. Someone very dear to her. She wished she could remember.

"You look so lovely I would like to introduce you to my friends. Will you come with me?"

"Let's finish our coffee first."

"Of course. I meant later."

As they walked down the boulevard the girl in the tight black leather dress that exposed half of her rounded bosom, took her arm. The girl's hair hung almost to her waist. She kept tilting her head to remove it from her eyes.

Milo was thinking she should put new rubber heels on her calf high black boots so they wouldn't click so noisily against the sidewalk. The young people sure dressed strange here in Los Angeles, not like . . . like where . . . she wondered?

They neared a red van. The side door slid open. "Get in, the girl ordered." Milo did not like the tone of her voice and tried to back away. "Help her guys." Two men lifted Milo into the van. One man got into the driver's seat. "Go! Get the hell out of here." The girl with the auburn hair ordered.

"Who are you?" Milo asked.

"That's none of your business, lady. More important is who you are." The fellow with the long red hair said. He had piercing black eyes and was wearing a gold earring. Milo thought the black eyes did not go with the red hair. He probably dyed it. The other man wore a black beard and had cold grey eyes. He also wore one earring and reminded Milo of a gypsy violinist she had once seen in a portrait. Where?

"Do you play the violin?" She asked the driver. "We are asking the question's here, Lady." The van shot forward almost throwing Milo from her side seat.

"Check her purse. Let's see her ID."

"It say's she is, Milo Farley." The girl in the tight black leather dress said.

"I don't think so. According to her profile she should be fifteen pounds heavier and have brown hair. She doesn't match this fax at all." The fellow who didn't play the violin said.

Milo had lightened her hair to beige blonde at John's suggestion, but she thought it better not to say so. Why would these people have a fax of her? Who were they?

"Where did you get this lady? You better tell us." The man with the long red hair asked, holding up her credit cards. "You better tell us we have ways of making you talk." Milo knew they did. She was frightened and began to shake.

"You are scaring her. Let me handle this." The girl said.

"Sure like you handled the last job. You killed the old lady. Give me that fax. Take off her hat." The driver reached back and grabbed the fax swerving the van as he did so. Maybe the police would stop them and Milo could scream.

The big burly fellow driving glanced back at Milo and back to the fax. "You botched it again, Sam." He scolded the girl.

"But she is checked in the hotel as Farley. She has all his credit cards and she is the right age." Sam said.

"Did you ever check the phone book? There are a lot of Farleys there. Once more lady. Who are you?"

Milo began to cry. "I am Vista Rubinoff from Ohio or is it Texas. I think it is Texas." She remembered. With the tears streaming down her face Vista turned to Sam. "You remind me of my granddaughter, Nickoel." It startled Vista so that she had remembered that she forgot to be afraid. "Will you write down what I just told you so I won't forget. Please I don't want to forget again."

"Thanks Sam. This one is really a loony tune. And her profile says she has no family." The man with the long red hair said. "You sure can pick 'em."

"Where did you get this billfold and credit cards?"

"I don't remember." And she didn't. She had forgotten all about John Farley and that she was a Milo Aroma once. She was Vista Rubinoff from Houston, Texas. She must hurry and call Nickoel, she would be worried about her.

"Put her out around the next corner. Keep the purse." The driver ordered.

"How about the hotel key?" Sam asked.

"Keep that too. We may want to pay the lady another visit."

"Can I keep her jewelry?" Sam asked.

"Hey we're not common thieves. We are in the people business. And give her the money too."

"You remind me of my granddaughter." Vista repeated.

"Sure Lady, whatever you say."

"We'll drive up to Farley's Mansion. Maybe he left the dossier hidden there. When we put the old lady out, put the landscaping signs on the van." George the burly driver said.

"I have a son named George." Vista said.

"Get her out of here."

"Okay! Okay! Do you mind stopping first?" The red headed fellow said.

"What is your name?" Vista asked.

"Never mind. You wouldn't have a son by my name." The door slid open and the red headed man lifted Vista to the ground. "It's Lucifer."

"No. I don't know anyone by that name. What day is this?" She asked.

"God Lady! Don't you know anything?"

"We'll see you later Lady." The bearded man said.

Vista walked to a corner news stand and bought a newspaper, so she would know the date. She was in a strange part of town. She could not remember where she was going this morning or where she was coming from. She walked into the lobby of a second rate hotel and asked where the phones were. She would call Nickoel and ask her to come and pick her up. She dialed 876-9707. "Hello! Macy's. extension please?"

CHAPTER SEVEN

A Wedding Postponed

It had been three months since Vista's disappearance. Some of the family had resigned themselves to the fact that she was dead.

It was late October. Between, Yom Kippur, Halloween, Thanksgiving and Christmas, plus a few birthdays and anniversaries which both families expected them to attend, Nathan was unsure as to when Nickoel would set a date. Their families were both spread out across the continent and their wishes had to be dealt with as well.

"Damn it, Nickoel, your grandmother is gone forever. I want us to get married." Nathan Golden was tired of waiting for their wedding date to be set. "Its been almost three months. They probably killed her when they killed her husband."

Nathan felt he had to be abrupt with Nickoel. Sooner or later she would have to face reality.

"She is not gone! I know she is alive somewhere."

"There are a lot of things that go unreported, especially in foreign countries." Nathan argued.

"She is alive Nathan and you will never change my mind." Nickoel began to cry.

"This thing is tearing you apart. If you don't start considering my feelings, it may break us up."

"If that's the way you feel. Go!" Nickoel screamed.

"Please, honey, I feel so bad for you and so helpless. I don't know what to do anymore. You stay by the phone all the time. You won't attend any parties or social functions You don't even attend your church anymore."

"I do. I stop and light a candle every afternoon on my way home from the office. What do you care, you're a Jew."

"I care that you don't care about anything anymore. Sometimes I think you don't even care about me?"

"I do, Nathan, I do. You know I do."

"I just want you to realize what this is doing to you, to us." Nathan took Nickoel in his arms and kissed her tear stained face. "I want you so much and you just don't seem interested anymore. Do you still want to marry me?"

"Yes. Of course. But not until I find grandmother."

Nathan could push her no further. Their mothers had all the arrangements made. All they had to do was set the date. Nathan had a big deal in computer chips coming up on the west coast, he would be gone for several weeks. Maybe she would miss him enough to go ahead with the wedding then.

"I love you Nickoel. I won't wait any longer." The door seemed to slam harder than usual when Nathan left. She would surely lose him if she didn't consent to marry him soon.

She left the room before her mother could tell her once again that Nathan was right. This time Esther followed her daughter to her room and watched while she played back her messages.

"You're wasting your time Nickoel, grandmother is dead."

"How can you say that! Your own mother."

Esther was trying to make Nickoel face reality. Doctor Elam had called that morning inquiring about Vista. He had told her that she was suffering from an advanced case of Alzheimer's disease.

"It's terrible to watch someone with a disease that you have no control over. To be with them, to take care of them and they don't even recognize their own family."

"I don't care. I would take care of her and protect her, the way she protects me from the storms. She is alive and I will find her," Nickoel ran down the stairs and into the garden. The leaves were falling and the summer flowers were withering. Why did she have to be reminded of death even here in the garden?

Esther Drum's hand trembled as she poured water from the tea pot. She could not hold back the tears. Was her dear mother alive somewhere and in need of her family?

James took the tea kettle from his mother and finished pouring the water for tea. His blond curls fell over his tanned forehead. His blue-green eyes met hers. She is gone Mother, we can't keep burning the candles for her forever."

"Don't say that, James. I never say this in front of Nickoel, but I believe she is alive and that she needs us."

"They have traced her half way around the world. You have heard how bad those countries are. I tell you Mother she is dead." Esther could see in his eyes that he did not believe what he was saying. "Okay, Mother. We will keep lighting candles at Saint Marks. Dear God. Don't let her suffer." They held hands across the table and wept silent tears.

Nickoel's phone rang. She answered it on the first ring. It was Nathan inviting her to go to California with him. She could put her calls on 'call forwarding'. "Damn it Nickoel. You are making my life miserable. I didn't want to leave on a sour note. You never can tell about these airplanes."

"Nathan, bite your tongue! I have enough to worry about."

"Just testing to see if you still care. I'll call you tonight."

CHAPTER EIGHT

Vista Finds A New Family

Vista shopped for makeup. A makeup artist from Est'ee Lauder cosmetics coaxed her into letting her do her make over. She sat on the high stool and watched in the mirror as the girl in the white smock applied foundation and rouge. "You have a lovely complexion." The girl said as she busied herself with more applications.

"I've been told that before." And she knew she had but who told her? Where? It was evening as she left the store. She guessed Fall was close. The days were growing shorter. She would have to find a hotel. She wondered where she had been staying?

"Your credit card please." The desk clerk asked.

"They were stolen today. Some young people stole my purse."

"How do you intend to pay?." He asked.

"Will cash be all right?"

"You will have to pay in advance."

Milo signed the register, Vista Conrad, her maiden name.

Tomorrow she would buy some new clothes, and a new hat. She always wore hats and she could not remember what had happened to hers. The days events had already been forgotten.

Vista left each morning, roamed the streets, and shopped. She did not feel happy and could not remember why.

She had been in the same hotel for several weeks, paying a few days each time in advance.

"Mrs. Conrad, you owe us for last week." The clerk said.

"I'll pay you soon." She was refused room service. The next day as she passed through the lobby she was escorted to the main desk.

"May we have your key please?" She gave them the key from her red purse. "Don't you have any other clothes? You have been wearing the same clothes for two weeks now. Don't you have a family? Why don't you call them? And why aren't you getting a Social Security check? You must be old enough. At least that would pay for your keep." The manager said.

Vista did not answer. She handed the key over and walked out into the bright sunlight and a new day on the boulevard.

It was late. She only had a few dollars left. Vista had no idea where she was going to sleep and she was getting tired. As she approached a corner news stand, she saw the front page of the evening news. A picture of an older man caught her eye. She stopped and picked up the paper. '*John Farley, U.S. Diplomat to Israel murdered. His new wife still missing*'. "Well, you going to buy or not, Lady?"

Vista did not answer. She handed him the money without taking her eyes from the picture. The man looked so familiar to her. Was he someone from her past?" She tore off the front page and put it in her purse. The rest of the paper she handed back to the newsman.

"Now, what am I supposed to do with this?"

"Throw it away, please."

"Do I look like the city trash collector?"

Vista walked away. After several blocks she found a Mc Donalds. She took her food to a back corner of the restaurant and ate slowly. She liked McDonalds. The people were friendly and they were always clean. She had been walking all after noon. After a little while she lay her head on her arms and fell asleep.

Around two A.M. A young man in uniform touched her shoulder. "Are you okay, Lady?"

"Yes! Yes! I came in for coffee. I must have fallen asleep." She said as she went in a daze to buy a cup of coffee.

When she came back she straightened the big brim of her red hat and took off her sun glasses. She placed them in her purse and took out a lipstick and mirror.

The young officer sat and watched her. "Isn't it quite late for you to be out alone?"

"I know, I missed the bus. I went to a late movie."

"Do you want me to drive you home?"

"No! That won't be necessary. The buses will start again soon."

"Not for another couple hours."

"That's okay. I'll wait."

"I still think it is dangerous for you to be out this time of night. Put your jewelry in your purse. This is not a neighborhood where you flash jewelry. You sure you don't want me to take you home?" Vista shook her head. The young officer left. He waved to her as he got into his car.

The next day Vista walked several blocks. She found a park just off the boulevard and whilst away the afternoon watching the children play.

As Vista watched she saw one father throw away half a bag of popcorn. She waited until he was out of sight then she retrieved it from the trash and ate it.

That evening she went back to the McDonalds. She watched for people to leave food on their trays. She ordered an orange juice with the last of her money. She took short walks around that part of town. Watching the people, window shopping and meandering in nearby parks, always returning to the warmth of the atmosphere of the McDonalds. She sat in the back corner where she wouldn't be conspicuous.

Again a tap on her shoulder. The same officer as last night questioned her. "Missed your bus again? Are you sure you have money."

He was soft spoken and had a warm smile that showed a beautiful set of the whitest teeth Vista had ever seen. She felt she could trust him. "No. I didn't miss the bus. And yes I have no money."

"He looked at her expensive jewelry. "You must have credit cards. They are no good to you here at McDonalds. I'll buy you some coffee." Her stomach lurched from hunger.

He returned with sandwiches, fries and apple turnovers. He watched as she ate. "Why are you here this time of morning?" Vista did not answer.

"I am a policeman. I am just finishing my shift. I worried about not taking you home last night. Are you sure you are all right?. You are wearing the same clothes you had on yesterday." Vista straightened her hat. "Are you having trouble at home? Are you running away? You don't look like a lady who should be out this time of morning."

"I am Andy Elias. What is your name?"

"Vista Conrad."

"I'll bet that is part of Buena Vista, which means beautiful view."

"When I was young, a long time ago."

"You still are and would be more so with a good nights sleep and a hot bath. You haven't been to bed for a couple days have you?" Vista dropped her eyes and shook her head.

"Do you have grandchildren?"

"Yes, several."

"Come, let me take you home."

"No!. I can't go home." Oh! Where was home, Vista wondered.

"Trouble at home. I thought so. We have a guest room why don't you come home with me. We have a new baby so you will have to make your own breakfast."

"Congratulations! Sounds like your wife could use some help. I'm healthy and strong and a good cook." At least she thought she was a good cook. She must be.

"We'll talk about it tomorrow. The hour is late, to quote Shakespeare." He slipped his arm in hers and led her to the car. He was such a pleasant fellow. Vista liked him very much.

Milo fell fast asleep in the comfortable seat of Andy's late model car.

It was a comfortable room, decorated in muted shades of lavender and pink. Vista slept late. The cries of the new baby awakened her. A terry cloth robe lay over the end of her bed. She showered, put on her makeup and followed the voices down the hall. As she neared the kitchen, she heard a woman's voice.

"Really, Andy, You have got to quit bringing home every stray you meet. We have a baby now to worry about. Someday you are going to get us all murdered in our beds. You don't know anything about the person you brought home last night." The voice said.

You'll like her. She's having trouble at home. She's been sleeping in McDonald's the last two nights."

"I swear Andy you're just like your father. You ethnic men are all alike. Why do I love you?" The baby began to cry.

"You could at least bring home someone young. What can an old lady do."

"I can rock the baby to sleep." Vista said entering the kitchen. "If you will allow me. I'm nice and clean, I just had a shower. May I?" Vista reached for the baby.

"Vista Conrad, my wife, Alice."

"Happy to meet you. Thank you Andy. The room is lovely.

What a beautiful baby. Is he finished nursing?" Alice sat with her mouth open and her breast exposed from where she had just been nursing the baby."

"Nursing is good for the baby but very tiring for the mother. You rest. I'll put the baby down." Vista said.

Andy laughed and Alice hurriedly placed her breast back in her bra. She threw a towel at Andy.

He went to the door and threw her a kiss. Get some rest, Honey. I want you to be in shape so we can make another baby tonight. Alice ran towards him like she was going to hit him. They embraced and kissed. Andy the policeman was a happy man. And he knew Vista and Alice liked each other.

"You enjoy your breakfast and a second cup of coffee with your husband. I'll rock the baby to sleep."

"Andy led Alice back to the table and poured her a second cup of coffee.

"You see, you shouldn't be so quick to judge. She's not that old." Andy said.

After the second lullaby the baby was asleep. Vista returned to the kitchen. "What a handsome boy."

"Just like his father." Andy bragged.

"Thank you for letting me stay. I will make it up to you some day." Vista said.

"You don't look homeless to me." Alice said her eyes taking in Vista's diamonds and gold jewelry.

"Alice!" Andy exclaimed.

"I heard what you said, Alice. I'm harmless and maybe I can help you for a few days. I'm a good cook." Vista hoped she was.

"Why not Alice? Vista is an answer to our prayers. Your mother was supposed to come from Michigan but she is ill with the flu." Andy added.

Vista left the room so they could decide what to do. She found a pink cotton house dress across her bed and knew that Alice had already consented to her staying.

"Vista returned to the kitchen. Andy had already left.

"You have a lovely singing voice, Vista."

"Thank you. What would you like me to do first?

"Just bring a cup of coffee and let's talk for awhile. Besides, anything you do would be an improvement on this place." Alice said referring to the sink full of unwashed dishes. A basket of baby laundry set next to the laundry room.

"Do you use Ivory Snow for the baby clothes?"

"No. Today we use Dreft." Alice knew it had been some time since Vista Conrad washed baby laundry.

That afternoon when Alice was napping, Vista went to the phone and dialed the number that was always on her mind.

876-9707.

"Hello! Joe's TV repair." Vista hung up. She was disappointed. She was expecting a sweet young voice.

CHAPTER NINE

Riches To Rags

Alice Elias was about the same size as Vista. She didn't seem to mind sharing her clothes with Vista.

One morning several weeks later Vista was at the sink. Andy slipped up behind her and kissed her on the back of the neck. "Oops, I thought you were Alice." Vista playfully smacked him with a wooden spoon. "Must be the clothes."

"Shame on you getting an old lady excited." Vista laughed.

Andy took her arm and led her to the table. "Sit down I want to talk to you." Andy watched her over the brim of his coffee cup. "You haven't once mentioned going home, or your family, Vista. You don't know who you are, do you?"

Vista's fading blue eyes met Andy's. "I only remember little things like farms and cows and lullaby's. And that I like to wear big hats and pretty clothes."

"I'm taking you shopping today. You have not been out of the house in a month. You seem happy, but I feel like we are taking advantage of you. I have checked the missing files and can not find anything on you. Will you promise to tell me if you remember anything? Your family must be frantic worrying about you." Andy said.

"You do too much for me. I don't want you spending money on me. You have shared your home and family with me. That's more than enough."

"I'm just going to buy you a new hat. We'll go to the big new mall. It will be fun. Then I will take you to lunch." Andy could see the delight on Vista's face. "You know we are very fond of you, Lady. Your family must be missing such a cheerful, happy woman as you, Vista." Andy continued.

"I hope so." Vista dropped her eyes avoiding Andy's concerned gaze.

"Are you sure your name is Vista Conrad."

"I think so."

"Is there any other name that comes to mind. I have been trying to find your family. I am a policeman you know."

It's my business to take care of lost people. You have no credit cards, no driver's license, do you remember your Social Security number?

"I told you, they were stolen. They were stolen twice."

"You remember that? Where? When?"

"I don't know. I just know it happened twice." Alice said placing her head in her hands.

"Don't worry. Don't fret, Vista. You have a home with us for as long as you like. We just want to make sure you are happy." Andy came around the table and put his arms around Vista.

"I am very happy, Andy. Very happy." And for the moment she was.

"I'll come to pick you up at eleven thirty. Be ready." He blew her a kiss. Then she heard his car drive down the lane.

It was a quiet neighborhood. Alice was in the nursery nursing the baby. Vista took her coffee out to the terrace.

She watched two blue birds in the tall pines. In one corner of the garden in an alcove surrounded by Eucalyptus bushes, stood a statue of the Virgin Mary. She walked over to the alcove and said a prayer for Nickoel. Yes, she had a granddaughter Nickoel in Houston. She would write it down to tell Andy when he came back. She felt safe and happy here in the garden among the beds of purple, red and pink petunias and yellow pansies that leaned toward the Virgin statue as though they too, were saying a prayer. Vista remembered a poem she had written on a day like this when Nickoel had helped her plant flowers in the garden.

> Little toe head girl so sweet
> Kneeling at her granny's feet,
> planting neatly in a row'
> Zinnias, Phlox and Four O'Clocks.
>
> That day would be remembered long
> Maybe even in a song
> A special day for just the two
> of Zinnias, Phlox and Four O'Clocks.
>
> Years passed she came from far away
> To see her granny this particular day
> She knelt beside her chair and whispered
> "Granny remember, the Zinnias, Phlox and
> Four O'Clocks."

Her Granny pulled her down to kiss,
For the last time her tender lips,
And whispered back, "Those were the days
of Zinnias Phlox and Four O'Clocks.

Her thoughts turned to a number. Andy had said she was old enough to collect Social Security. She wished she could remember for Andy's sake."

As they drove to the mall Vista started reading the street signs. "Cherry Street. I am going to live on Cherry Creek Lane."

"Is that your address Vista?" Andy asked.

"Not yet. It's going to be. I am supposed to live there with my husband."

"You have a husband. What's his name?" Andy tried not to act too excited, he did not want to alarm Vista.

"James, maybe John. I'm not sure Andy."

"That's okay. I know where that street is. It's way over in Cherry Valley, close to San Bernardino. After Lunch we will take a ride over there."

Andy laughed and teased her in the lingerie department. The sales girls loved his clowning. "How about this Vista?" He said holding up a black lace teddy.

"Who is the lovely lady you call, Vista?" The sales girl asked.

"She's my mistress." Vista gave him a scornful look. "No, she's my mother." Andy said as he hugged her.

"It's nice to see such an attentive son." She replied.

They decided on blue silk pajamas and a robe to match.

"Now for a new hat." Andy said taking her arm and escorting her to the hat department.

"A Chapeau for my Lady Fair." he said to the sales clerk, extending his credit card.

Vista decided on a large brimmed navy straw. Andy agreed that it made her look taller. She decided to wear it and handed her red one to the clerk to bag. She picked up her purse and sun glasses as Andy guided her to the dress department. "But you said you were just going to buy a hat." Vista protested.

"So, I lied. You are so great to shop for. I wish I could buy you the whole store. You look great in everything."

"You pick out a few dresses and I will be right back and pay for them. I want to call Alice and see if she and the baby are okay."

Vista went around the racks of dresses. She got turned around and became disoriented. The racks of dresses seemed to strike out at her. The rustling of the dress fabrics frightened her and made her want to get away from them. She backed out into the isle and almost backed down the escalator. A man caught her arm and steadied her." He was a store detective. "Are you okay lady?"

"Yes. I am fine," she said and put her trembling hand on the escalator rail. She went down to the first floor and out the front door.

A bus was waiting there. She got on just before the bus pulled away from the curb. "This bus to Hollywood." The driver said as Vista took her seat. "Hey lady, that will be eighty cents. Only because you are a senior citizen. Everyone else pays more."

"Yes. Wait a minute. Vista regained her composure. She put her bags down and took the correct change from her purse. Vista forgot all about Andy and the family she had for such a short time. "Gorman's Theater" The bus driver called out. The name sounded familiar to Vista so she got off the bus.

She had money in her pocket that someone had given her, but she couldn't remember who. The theater would not open for it's matinee for another hour. Vista went into a coffee shop and ordered coffee and cheese cake. She ate slowly wondering where she got all the packages. She opened them one by one and was surprised at the contents. Only the red hat looked vaguely familiar. She spent all afternoon in the theater. When she came out it was evening. She was hungry. She went again to the same coffee shop and ordered a tuna sandwich.

XXX

Andy returned to the dress department and found Vista gone.

He went back to the hat and lingerie departments thinking she may have gone back there. "Where is the lady I was with?" he asked. No one had seen which way she went. Andy ran about the store frantically looking for Vista. He even had them page her. Nothing. It was like she had disappeared off the face of the earth.

He searched the store, the street, other shops in the shopping center. He searched for several hours. He had to leave, it was time for him to go to work.

"I lost her, Alice. I couldn't find her anywhere." His voice broke.

"Maybe she returned to her family."

"I don't think she has a family. Damn! Alice, I only left for a few minutes to call you."

"That was hours ago. She has been lost all this time?.

"Yes."

"She will call. I'll tell her to take a cab. Try not to worry, Dear." Andy did not tell Alice that he suspected she had alzheimers.

"I've grown very fond of that lady, Alice."

"I know, Andy. We all love her. She is so easy to love. We'll find her. Go to work."

That night Andy stopped at McDonalds, hoping to find Vista sleeping there. He wished he had given her more money.

What could have happened to her? It was late but he stopped by the Church to light a candle for Vista. Maybe he didn't try hard enough to find out her identity, but she seemed so happy with them.

The hours and days drug by. Andy put out a missing persons bulletin and alerted the other police shifts to watch for her.

"I can't believe she just disappeared, Alice. How? Where?"

XXX

Vista was asked to leave an all night restaurant. She got tired and lay down in a deep dark doorway. By the weeks end, she was hungry and broke. Her hair was matted. She put on her lipstick, straightened her big hat and sun glasses and roamed the Hollywood streets. No one seemed to pay much attention to her.

One night she picked a deep recessed doorway and settled down to sleep. "Hey you! Get out of there. That's my place." A crass voice said. "I've seen you around. Go home. You don't belong in these streets." The big woman said it, like she personally owned the streets of Hollywood.

"No! Vista said. "I'm hungry you got anything to eat?" She said, looking at the old woman's cart.

"What do I look like, the Salvation Army?"

She made Vista leave. Vista found another doorway and went to sleep. The next day she found the big fat street woman and followed her as she pushed her cart down the side streets.

The woman went down Vine street, crossed over several other streets and went into a park. She sat down on a park bench. She took out a half eaten sandwich. Vista sat down beside her. "Get away, I don't want you following me around. You're getting to be a real pest."

"Please, I'm so hungry." She straightened her big hat and put her sun glasses on. Vista was still carrying the bags from last week. She handed one to the woman. "I'll give you this for that sandwich." She said, handing the bag from Macy's to the street woman.

The woman pulled out the blue silk pajamas that Andy had bought for her. "Just where do you think I am going to wear this?" Vista took it back and offered her the bag with the red hat. "That's better." She put the red hat on and strutted around her cart like she was a movie star. Posing this way and that. Vista could not help laughing at her.

The woman searched through her cart and handed Vista a sandwich, which she wolfed down. "You really are a hungry one."

"What's your name?"

"I don't know. What's yours?" Vista said her mouth full of food.

"Just call me Ruby. I'm a jewel. How come you don't know your name? Did you hit your head or something? I ain't never seen you around before."

"I don't know and don't ask me again. Just leave me alone." Vista did not like the tone of the street woman's voice.

"Hah. Leave me alone, and the big hat and sun glasses.

You got a name. I christen you, Greta Garbo."

"Who's that?"

"Never mind. Why are you hungry? Anyone with all that jewelry shouldn't be hungry." Ruby said grabbing Vista's hand in her grubby one.

"Vista drew back her hand. "Leave me alone." Vista was not sure she liked the dirty woman.

"If you give me one of those rings, we can both eat good for a week." Ruby said pointing to Vista's hand. Ruby was afraid to touch her again. Vista reminded her of a little animal that was cornered and ready to strike out.

"You will feed me?"

"Like a mother taking care of her child." Ruby chided

Vista took off a diamond and emerald dinner ring and placed it in Ruby's dirty palm. Here help me push the cart, Greta. We're gonna eat good tonight." They walked down Holly wood boulevard, the rims of their big hats bouncing as they walked.

They entered a nice restaurant. The white table clothes and candles reminded Vista of some place she had been before. She wished she could remember where. Ruby asked to see the owner. "He's busy." A tall middle aged woman with black hair and sorrowful eyes said,

"You just tell him Ruby's here. He'll see me."

A pot bellied bald headed man came out of the back room. "What is it Ruby?"

"I got something pretty to show you. Ain't that the prettiest thing you ever saw?" She asked, extending the ring in her outstretched palm.

"Where did you get it?"

"I found it in the middle of the street. Big as you please. Yes sir. It's not a hot item. You know Ruby never brings you anything stolen."

The man made Ruby an offer. "That ain't even half what it's worth. It would look mighty pretty on the misses' finger."

"He spotted Vista standing in the doorway. "Who's your friend?"

"Greta Garbo, She want's to be alone. You want the ring or shall I take it down to Jake's bar and show it around. I like this place. It's classier for my new friend. Tell you what. I'll take the cash offer and you allow us both to eat dinner here for a whole week."

"Only if you come in through the alley."

"I can't park my cart back there. Someone will steal it."

"You can bring it inside the back door. And you can set in the back booth."

"It's a deal." Ruby placed the ring in his pudgy hand.

"We will be at the back door in a few minutes, make sure the help lets us in." Ruby pocketed the cash and never bothered to give any of it to Vista.

"How much further?" Vista asked hanging on to the cart.

"Just around the next corner, Honey. It sure was my lucky day runnin' into you, Greta. I suppose you'll be a passel of trouble though." She added.

Ruby and Vista ate all they could. They left by the back door and went around to the deep recessed door on Hollywood Boulevard.

As they rounded the corner Vista felt sick and began to vomit. Ruby took her to the curb. Vista vomited up all she had eaten. "You ate too much, too fast. How long has it been since you have eaten?"

"I don't know."

"Don't you know anything, Greta?"

"No. Just leave me alone."

"I got to get you to the doorway before the police come along and pick us up." Ruby put her in the back of the doorway and gave her a dirty pillow that she pulled from her cart. She took a belt from around her waist and tied one end to her wrist and the other around the cart and laid down in front of Vista. "Thieves. You got to be careful in this neighborhood." She explained to the uncaring Vista. Ruby began snoring the minute she laid down.

Vista felt her finger for the missing ring as she lay in the dark doorway. It took her awhile to get used to the hard pavement. She felt safe tucked away behind the oversized Ruby.

"Now eat slow." Ruby ordered Vista. "We got all day. The oatmeal and orange juice will settle your stomach."

Vista felt better after breakfast. They walked along pushing the grocery cart. They walked several blocks to a park. They sat on a bench watching the children at play.

Vista began humming lullabies and swinging her folded arms as though she had a baby in them. She stopped to tell Ruby that you should wash the baby's clothes in Dreft.

"You're a funny one. Is that all you know. Sing something popular." Ruby ordered.

Vista broke into *I'm Forever Blowing Bubbles*, and Ruby joined in with her raspy coloratura voice.

"You got a nice voice Greta. Maybe I should be your agent and sign you up for the movies. I sure would like to know who you really are."

"None of your business, Miss Ruby."

"Stop talking nasty to me. If it had not been for old Ruby, you would have died of starvation. You ain't got no cause to get mad at me. Now have you?"

"I just don't like you bossing me around and I am not going to play in any of your old movies."

"Okay, settle down. You got that forgetten' disease or you got a mighty hard whop to your head. I'm gone to watch the papers. There may be a big reward for you. Ever think of that?"

"Maybe." Vista went into a rendition of *Over The Rainbow*. Ruby did not join in. She sat back on the park bench picking her rotted teeth and watching Vista.

"I can tell, you come from class. The way you act and talk. I may not be the only jewel on this here park bench."

The next day Ruby sold Vista's gold watch. "You're a walking gold mine, Greta. You're not like the other street people. Yes sir. I like you, Greta Garbo. I'd probably take care of you if you didn't have all that jewelry. You're just a very likeable person."

"I like you too, Ruby. You have been very good to me. I won't forget you."

But just the same Ruby kept her close. She never let Vista out of her sight for a minute. Maybe she was afraid someone else would take her away. Ruby knew she was no ordinary street person. She would just have to take care of her.

The weeks passed. Vista's jewelry had all been sold or traded for food, and still Ruby took care of Vista. "You are becoming a liability," she told her one day. "It's hard to beg food for two of us and you're no help." It's just like having a youngun' to feed and take care of.

Vista didn't look like she had been well taken care of. Her big hat was frayed around the edges. She hadn't had a bath in weeks. The last time they went to the shelter Ruby was upset with Vista because she became too friendly with the other street people. She was jealous of Vista's talking to anyone else.

Vista had lost twenty pounds and her eyes were sunk back in her head. They weren't happy and snappy anymore. She seldom answered Ruby's questions. She just followed her along stopping at times to rest. Ruby would look back and find her sitting on a curb. She would turn around and go back for her.

"Get up from the curb, Greta. A police car is comin' They'll take you to jail. Hurry! get up. Here hold onto the cart. As long as we keep moving they won't bother us but you can't sit down, especially on the curb. They call that loitering or is it littering, whatever. I sure have to watch your every move. It's very unsettlin' at my age to have to take care of another person." Ruby complained.

Vista's steps were getting slower and more unsteady. Every step became an effort. She was so dirty no one would recognize her.

One morning Ruby tried to wake Vista, "Greta, Greta! Oh! please don't be dead. I'll miss you. Don't leave me Greta." Tears were streaming down Ruby's dirty cheeks. Vista moaned. "Please, someone help me she's dying!" Ruby screamed. No one paid any attention. Finally a policeman heard Ruby's screams and came to see what was wrong.

"Who is she?" He asked.

"Greta. Greta Garbo."

"Sure." The policeman said. He went to the corner and called for an ambulance.

"I'm going with you." Ruby said to the ambulance men.

"And leave your cart here in the middle of Hollywood Boulevard?" The policeman asked.

"I don't care. She's my only friend and she needs me." Ruby said, tears streaking her dirty cheeks.

"Okay. But the hospital will throw you out, you're so dirty. You are on your own. I can't help you." He shook his head.

The sirens screeched as Ruby's dirty hand held Vista's small feverish one. "Don't die Greta. Please don't die."

CHAPTER TEN

The Mountain Mansion

It had been several weeks since Vista went shopping with Andy Elias, where she disappeared from the department store. A day did not pass that Andy and Alice did not talk about her.

"I left a note on the door of that home on Cherry Creek Lane. You would think someone would have called us." Andy complained.

"Why don't you take another ride down there and see if anyone has come back to the house?." Alice suggested.

"I would take you and the baby along for the ride, but I never know who or what I may get involved in."

"That's all right, Andy, I have a lot of house work.

I hope you find Vista. You have not been yourself since she disappeared." Alice said, a sad note in her voice.

As Andy drove south on 101 towards San Bernardino, his thoughts turned to the day after Vista disappeared and his trip to San Bernardino to find the house on Cherry Creek Lane.

The house set like a large jewel on the side of the mountain. The afternoon setting sun brought out the muted lavenders, pinks and burnt orange colors in the stones of the mansion. Two huge bronze lions guarded the front entrance. The view of the Valley was breathtaking. It had been evening then and the sunset that evening was one he would remember always. There was no one around the mansion. The grounds were manicured, but no sign of a gardener or care-taker. He wondered if he would find everything the same and would his note still be in the brass door knocker on the front door.

It was noon when Andy arrived on Cherry Creek Lane. The houses were far apart and built in the hollows of the winding mountain side. He found his note still in the front door. The flowers and shrubs had been trimmed. Someone must be taking care of the mansion while the owner was away. He walked around to the back, opened the gate to the pool area and crossed to the sliding glass doors. He peered in. Everything seemed to be the same as before. There had been no mail in the mail box so he could not find a name to go with the house.

There were other homes on the winding mountain road. The owners had all been home, but they did not know anyone by Vista's description. Nor did they know anything about the mansion at 4355 Cherry Creek Lane. They believed that a man lived there alone and that he traveled a lot. It was the only house left on Cherry Creek Lane so Andy just assumed this must be the home Vista was talking about. Why should he believe her? She was not sure about anything else. Maybe he was on a wild goose chase. Maybe he should check with the court house records to see who owned the property.

Andy tried the doors. None were open. He wondered if touching the doors would set off the alarm. He went around to the side. Lavender and pink oleander bloomed along the path.

There was a small patio that overlooked a steep cliff.

Not a good place for children or drunks, Andy thought. He tried the door that led into the kitchen area. He lifted the top on the gas grill. He found a key. The key opened the door. Andy held his breath as he cautiously entered the house. It had always bothered him to enter silent houses. You just never knew what you might find. In his years of experience it was always a good idea to go in with your gun ready for action. Andy pulled out his gun and called out, "Is anyone home?" There was no answer. His voice echoed through the vacant house. Andy went to the front of the house and at the foot of a marble circular stairs he called out again.

Andy opened doors to a large dinning room. The crystal chandelier glistened in the morning sunlight. Andy had never seen such a beautiful home. He checked all the rooms on the first floor and was half way up the marble stair case, when a voice called out. "Who goes there?"

"Police Lieutenant, Andy Elias."

A man came from the back foyer. "Let me see your credentials."

Andy brought out his badge and extended it to the man at the bottom of the stairs. The man looked at it and lowered his gun. "What are you doing here? A little out of your precinct aren't you?"

"I'm looking for the man who lives here. I am looking for a missing person."

"The man who lives here was murdered several weeks ago in Israel."

"Oh my God! I'm looking for a woman, his wife maybe. The woman I'm looking for disappeared last month."

"He did have a new wife. Seems she disappeared in Israel without a trace." The man said.

"What did she look like? Do you have a picture of her?"

"Just the one that was in the newspaper. My wife cut it out. I caught two young fellows here last month. They were going through the place. They are being held for questioning."

"Where? Maybe they know about Vista."

"They are at the Valley jail. Who is this Vista?"

"Before I tell you anything else, I want to know who you are?" Andy said.

"I'm Cecil Anthony. I have been working for Mr. Farley for several years. I take care of the place when he is gone." The gray haired man said as he took his pipe from his pocket and lit it.

"Some place." Andy said.

"It's the prettiest one on this mountain range."

"You say Mr. Farley got married recently?"

"Yes, but her name wasn't, Vista. I was real surprised when he called me from San Francisco to tell me he was getting married. He left me orders to follow, to make her arrival special. I even got to talk to her over the phone. She seemed very pleasant. Mr. Farley had been widowed for more then twelve years. Wait, I got something on his desk."

They went down a wide hallway and entered an elegant office. It had a white marble fireplace and was furnished with burnt leather tooled furniture. Cecil pulled the drapes to expose a breathtaking view of Cherry Valley.

"Who is Mr. Farley?" Andy asked.

"He was a foreign diplomat. I can't believe he is dead."

"Did he leave any letter or notes in the last month or so?" Andy asked.

Only the one to me about what to prepare for Mrs.

Farley's home coming. And one that he told me to give to his attorney if anything happened to him. But Pete Dial has been away for a month on vacation abroad."

"It is not addressed to anyone. Let's open it. There may be something in it to help me find my lady. And why would he be worried that something was going to happen to him?"

"I don't know. I've been working for him for a long time and that is the first time he ever said that. Maybe it was because he was getting married that he became more cautious."

"It's what Mr. Farley told me. I don't know."

"I am here in the capacity of missing persons. I think it would be all right since we are opening it together." Andy said.

Cecil Anthony handed the envelope to Andy.

To Whom It May Concern;

I am marrying a lovely lady who calls herself, Milo Aroma. I am very much in love with her. I want whoever reads this to know my feelings.

She seems to have no family. I don't believe Aroma is her real name. She seems to be in very good health.

I met her a few days after she was knocked down by two men who snatched her purse. I witnessed this and saw her hit her head. I don't believe it is amnesia. I have a feeling it is more than this. I intend to take her to the doctor when we return to the States from Israel. I write this because

I am worried about her future.

She has completely enchanted my life.

I have no other relatives. I want her to have everything I own except the little house in the Valley which I want to go to my friend

*Cecil Anthony. I also want Cecil Anthony to have $100,000
dollars from my account at the Fargo Bank.'*

Andy stopped reading and looked over at Cecil. "Aren't you glad
we opened this letter?" Andy asked.

The middle-aged man sat down in a big leather chair by the
fireplace. He was stunned. Andy read on.

*I am an only child and my parents were only children so I
have no living relatives.*

I am writing this because of my new wife.

*My friend Judge Joseph Finkel of San Francisco knows of my
desires in this matter. When you find out her real name, please
inform him.* I have left further instructions with Cecil
*Anthony. My will is with the Judge. I expect you, George, to take
care of my estate.*

Thank you for your consideration in this matter.

Sincerely,

John Farley

P.S. Milo was always dialing a telephone number
876-9707. *Sometimes she speaks of Ohio. But I notice a distinct
Texas twang at times. I intend to find the area code for that number
when we return. It is the only clue as to who my wife may be.'*

Andy wrote down the number and handed the letter back to
Cecil who still looked like he had the wind knocked out of him.

It seemed to Andy there would be legal entanglements. But
right now all he cared about was Vista. "Could I see that newspaper
article you talked about?" Andy asked.

"My wife has it at home."

"Please, let me follow you to your home. I must see it."

"Yes. Of course." Cecil replied, tapping his pipe gently on the pillar of the front portico. The look of disbelief still on his face.

Are the phones working? I want to call my wife to tell her I found a clue."

"By the way, the key in the barbecue grill, not a good idea, hide it somewhere else or take it home with you." Andy added as he dialed Alice. "Alice, how is the baby? Good. I want you to find the telephone bill for last month. I want to check the phone numbers. I think I am on to something. See you soon, Love." Andy hung up.

The picture was not very good. The woman's face was almost hidden by a big hat. "May I take this. I will send it back to you? I want my wife to see it."

Andy did not do much day dreaming on the way home. He was anxiously thinking about the telephone number in his pocket. It was late afternoon when he pulled up the drive to find Alice and the baby waiting for him. "Did you find anything?" Alice asked. Andy handed her the front page news story.

The caption under the picture read. "*John Farley Foreign Diplomat was found shot to death in a back street of the port city of Haifa, Israel. His new bride is still missing.' The bride, Milo Aroma and John Farley were married here in San Francisco by Judge Joseph Finkel.'*

"But our lady is Vista Conrad. Why are you showing me this?"

"Just wait there is more, much more. This Farley is a very wealthy man. He left a letter to whom it may concern. He said in the letter he was not sure that Aroma was her real name. Seems two thugs knocked her down and snatched her purse. She hit her head when she fell. But Mr. Farley said he thought it was something more serious than amnesia. He also said she kept dialing a telephone number. This one." Andy handed Alice the telephone number.

"So what does that mean?" Alice asked.

"That if she dialed that number from our phone, then we are looking for a Mrs. Farley, re; Milo Aroma, re; Vista Conrad. Someone at that number must know her."

"Andy you're late for work."

"I took the day off. I'm close to finding her, Alice. I can feel it. I believe she is a victim of alzheimers, and that she still has periods of remembering her past."

"But everyone is looking for her, the police, the F.B.I. and for sure the secret service, since she was in a foreign country. What makes you think you can find her?" Alice asked.

"Because, they don't care about her, the way I do. And they don't have this number."

"Why don't you give the number to them, they have secretaries and computers. They could do it better than you." Alice said. "And quicker."

"I want to try first. I will give it to them tomorrow."

Andy called the various area codes in Ohio. Columbus, Cleveland, and Cincinnati. He got a radio station, a book store and 'The Pet Set', a pet shop in Columbus.

The letter said, maybe Texas. First Andy tried Dallas and Fort Worth then Houston. It was seven o'clock in Houston. A sweet young voice answered.

"Hello, I'm calling from Los Angeles. I'm a police lieutenant and I'm trying to locate a missing person. My wife and I know her as Vista Conrad."

"Oh! My God! My Grandmother! She is alive." The girl began screaming at the other members of her family to pick up phones in other parts of the house, so they could hear as well.

Please give me your number in case we get cut off. Mr. We have been looking for months for Grandmother Vista. Is she all right? Mother! Uncle George! Everyone! Get on the phone." Nickoel called out.

"I don't know. You see I lost her several weeks ago when I took her shopping at Macy's. I went to call and check on my wife and new baby. When I got back to the department where I left her, she was gone."

Now it was Andy's turn to call out. "Alice get on the extension. I have Vista's family on the phone." Alice was surprised.

"Please tell me about Grandmother. The last we heard she was in Israel." Nickoel said.

"Someway she got to Los Angeles. It seems her husband Mr. Farley had suspicions that she may not be well." Andy told them about the letter Mr. Farley had left behind at the mountain Mansion.

"I know. We know. We found out too late that she has an advanced case of Alzheimer disease. She did a good job of hiding the truth from us."

"We love your grandmother." Alice said. "She came to live with us and helped me with our new baby. She seemed so happy."

"I found her sleeping in McDonalds. I knew she was not a street person. I took her home. I hoped after a few days I would find a missing person's file on her. I never did."

"But I filed one in San Francisco." Nickoel argued.

"Under what name."

"Milo Aroma and Vista Rubinoff."

"I was looking for a Conrad. Was your grandmother married to a John Farley?"

"Yes. We found that out and I went to Israel to try to find her." Nickoel answered. "I spent three weeks there."

"She has been here in Los Angeles." Andy said.

"How did you find me?" Nickoel asked.

"Mr. Farley left a number, but no area code. He said his wife kept dialing that number. So I began to call cities across the country."

"That's my private number. Grandmother remembered. Oh Mother, I miss her so." and she began to cry softly on the phone. "Mother are you listening to all this?"

"Yes, Dear, I am on the kitchen phone. Lieutenant Elias, you will call us the minute you hear anything, won't you?" Esther Conrad asked. "I am her daughter Esther Conrad."

"You probably don't know it, but your mother is a very rich widow. When we find her, I would advise you to bring your attorney as well."

"Lieutenant we are only interested in finding my mother. Money is of no importance without her."

"I am leaving on the next plane." Nickoel added.

"I don't think that is wise. My department is doing all they can to find her. That lady means a lot to Alice and me. Now that I have all the names, I'm sure it won't be long."

"Thank you for calling Lieutenant Elias. We are happy to know she returned from Israel." George said.

"At least we know she is still alive somewhere." Esther added.

"I'll keep in touch. Good night." Andy hung up. He neglected to tell them about the two men who had been rummaging through the house on the mountain. What had they been looking for? Andy wondered.

Tomorrow he would go to the Valley jail and question them. Perhaps they had seen Vista. Were they looking for her too?. Would they harm her?

CHAPTER ELEVEN

The Family Reunited

Nathan Golden had tried everything to get Nickoel to go ahead with their wedding. He even threatened to break off the engagement. How could he fight such loyalty? How could he go against the thing he loved most about her? She would surely be a loyal wife if he could ever make it happen. These were his thoughts as he winged his way to Los Angeles and the most important business meeting of his career. Nathan fingered the black onyx and diamond friendship ring that Nickoel had given him last Christmas. "Now, you won't need worry beads. Just rub the black onyx and all your worries will dissipate." she had said playfully. Wouldn't it be wonderful if life were that simple. He tried to put thoughts of her out of his mind, so he could concentrate on tomorrow's meeting. His micro chips were far superior to anything yet invented. Tomorrow he would prove it.

At Bethesda Hospital, the lady in room 807 had become a topic of conversation throughout the hospital.

"She's really a lovely lady. I wonder who she really is? Such nice manners." Nancy the attending nurse said as she came around the nursing station. "She insists on wearing that big hat in bed and those large sunglasses. She's really funny. That dirty street woman calls her, Greta Garbo. It sure does suit her."

The newspapers picked up on the story and Vista, alias Greta Garbo, was on the front pages of the Los Angeles papers. There was a large picture of Vista in the hospital bed wearing the big hat and sun glasses. *'Greta Garbo in Hospital.*

The caption read; 'A street person suffering from malnutrition and known to the hospital as Greta Garbo, because she mimics the old time star. No one seems to know her real identity. Nurse Gloria Michaels said. She keeps asking them to dial a telephone number.

"Oh my God! It's Vista. I know it." Nathan Golden exclaimed spilling his coffee as he ran from the hotel coffee shop to find the nearest telephone.

"Please! I know the lady called Greta Garbo. Keep her until I can come for her."

"You and seventy five others mister get in line." The hospital hung up.

Nathan called back. "Listen, I intend to pay her bill. She is my fiancee's grandmother."

"You're the third person today who claims to know her and want's to pay her bill."

Please take my name and keep her until I can get there."

"Don't worry, Mister, she isn't going anywhere. Besides she is good publicity for the hospital." Again she hung up.

Nathan called to postpone his meeting and then he called Nickoel. "Nickoel. I have good news."

"I know, I am looking at her. She is on the front page of the Houston Chronicle. Oh! Nathan, she's been trying to call me. I'm coming right away. I will arrive around three o'clock your time. I'm going straight to the hospital. See you there. I love you, Nathan."

Nathan had not been able to say a word. He was happy for Nickoel. Now they could be married.

XXX

Lieutenant Elias called his wife, Alice. "Have you seen the newspaper, Alice? I'm on my way to the hospital. I'll call you soon as I know what is happening with Vista."

"Call me as soon as you can. Hurry Andy." Alice took the baby to the nursery and sang the lullabies that had echoed through the house a month ago. Tears of joy wet the babies blonde curls.

"I'm Lieutenant Elias. I want to see the woman in 807."

"For a street woman she sure has lots of friends." The receptionist scrutinized Andy over the top of her silver rimmed glasses.

"What do you mean?"

"Several men have called or came in wanting to pay her bills."

"Don't worry. I am not rich but I will pay her hospital bill."

Lieutenant Elias went to the bed and hugged and kissed Vista. "I'm so glad you are okay. I have looked everywhere for you."

"Who are you?" The dissipated woman in the bed asked.

"I'm Andy. You took care of our new born baby. Don't you remember? I lost you in the department store."

Andy stood holding her hand and looking down at the shrunken lady in the bed and feeling guilty that he had let her get in this condition.

"Baby. Sounds familiar." Vista pushed Andy away and straightened her tattered hat.

"I bought that hat for you. Please try to remember." Andy was willing her to remember. Tears wet his eyes.

"I think so." Vista said not wanting to disappoint the good looking policeman.

I bought her this hat a month ago." He looked up from his kneeling position at the circle of nurses around the bed.

"Mother Vista! Where have you been?" Again Vista's hat was knocked askew by the young man hugging her. She pushed him away and straightened her hat. "Does she always act this way? I have never known Mother Vista to push anyone away. Do you think she is mad at me?" Nathan asked the nurses.

"I doubt that she even knows who you are." A heavy set nurse answered. "She is in a state of shock from the malnutrition, plus her Alzheimer has probably advanced since the last time you saw her."

"Who are You?" Nathan asked the policeman, as the news camera's clicked.

"I am Lieutenant Andy Elias. Vista lived with us for a month and helped my wife take care of our new baby. She seemed quite happy. I took her shopping and lost her in the department store. I had no idea she was afflicted with Alzheimer. I tried to find her family but I could find no missing person's file on her. I'm sorry."

"You were using her as a nanny?"

"I was giving her a home. I found her sleeping in McDonalds."

"You are a policeman. How did you miss the missing person's file?"

"We had no such report. At first we thought she was having family problems. We had no idea she was ill. She seemed so . . . normal.

Sal came strutting into the room. She had tried to clean up. She was wearing Greta's navy blue dress that was two sizes too small causing the button's to threaten to pop off. A gold front tooth lit up the smile in her old wrinkled face. "I was afraid you was dead, Greta. Who are these men?"

"My friends."

"Greta, I am your friend, your only friend."

"Who is this awful woman?" Nathan asked the nurses.

"She is a street person who has been taking care of her." Andy answered.

"Why didn't you turn Vista over to the police. You knew she couldn't be a street person." Nathan was angry and he didn't like the looks of the dirty street woman. "We have been looking for her for months."

"If she was yours, then you should of taken better care of her. She is my friend now and I will take care of her. Old Ruby watched over her real good."

"Get her out of here." Andy spoke rough and pointed his finger towards the door. Nobody moved. Maybe they thought Andy should take the lead since he was a policeman. "And besides how could you pay her hospital bill."

"Don't you worry mister. Ruby knows her rights. There are Public funds that take care of people like us."

"Mother Vista is not one of you. She is a lady and lives in a fine home. Now you get out of here."

I won't. Greta is my friend. And friends take care of each other."

Nathan had missed the most important business meeting of his career and he was in no mood to argue with this ugly person. "Officer, send her on her way."

Ruby continued, "She was my friend and a good one too. She wasn't doin' no harm. I was goin' to turn her in after her money and jewelry ran out, but I liked her and I just couldn't give her up"

"You sold all her jewelry?" Nathan asked taking Vista's hand in his.

"We had to eat Mister. Who are you anyway?"

"I'm her future grandson-in-law."

The nurse asked everyone to leave. There were more arguments.

"What's going on in room 108 is better than any fiction novel. I like her spunk. And that street person, Ruby, she's really something." Nurse Rob said to the intern, Doctor Kline.

"The patient needs rest. We must not let anymore news cameras in there today." Doctor Rob said emphatically.

Andy went to the phone and called Alice. "She has a family Alice. She is suffering from Alzheimer disease."

"That can't be true. She took such good care of baby Andy."

"I guess that came naturally, after all she is a mother and grandmother." Andy said in a strained voice.

"Andy, promise you won't bring home anymore strangers."

Andy promised, but Alice knew there would be other strangers sleeping in the guest room. Her Andy was a man who cared and Alice loved him deeply.

That evening Nickoel entered her grandmother's hospital room. She ran to her and hugged and kissed her. The months of not knowing her grandmother Vista's whereabouts was over. Tears streamed down her face. "Oh Grandmother! I knew you were alive!"

"Why are you crying Esther? Everything is all right."

"Grandmother, I am Nickoel." Vista straightened her hat ignoring what Nickoel had just said.

"Please don't cry, Esther. Mother is here."

Nickoel accepted the fact that her grandmother thought she was her mother Esther. She was just happy she had been found. She would take her home and nurse her back to health. Soon she would remember their time together.

CHAPTER TWELVE

A Wedding

A picture of Nathan kissing grandmother Vista in her hospital bed graced the front pages of every newspaper in Los Angeles.

"Now that I'm a celebrity, I suppose you will be anxious to marry me." Nathan teased Nickoel.

"It's over. Finally after all these months. Now we can go on with our lives." Nickoel crossed the room and into Nathan's arms. They kissed and looked out over the Pacific Ocean from their hotel room. "I wonder how soon we can take her back to Texas?" Nickoel continued.

The phone rang. It was the executives from the company that Nathan was supposed to meet that morning. "They want me to meet them at nine o'clock tomorrow." He turned to Nickoel.

"I sure messed up for the company. It will probably mean my job."

"I'm sorry Nathan."

As Nathan entered the conference room of the executive suite, the eight men that were waiting for his arrival stood up and applauded. Nathan was center stage and was not sure how to react. He was also a bit embarrassed. The president motioned to the chair at his right and Nathan sat down. Not quite sure what to do or say next. "Our man of the hour. A man who takes personal relationships to be more important than his own job or his company's desires." Nathan had a strange feeling that they may be making sport of him. After all these were not the 'good old boys' he was used to dealing with in Texas. They were sophisticated and treacherous from what he had heard from other executives. Well, he wouldn't stay here and be humiliated. He got up picked up his briefcase but before he could open the door the president had his arm around his shoulder. "Where are you going? I thought you were here to show us the new micro chip?"

"You are still interested?"

"Of course. Are you ready to show us?"

Nathan went back to the table and when he was finished he had a contract for ten million dollars worth of his company's micro chips.

"Well, when are you going to tell me about what happened at your meeting?" Nickoel asked.

"After we see Mother Vista. I am going to take you to the fanciest French restaurant in Los Angeles."

"Are we celebrating or is this the big build up for a bigger let down?"

"Just wait."

As the candle light flickered on Nickoel's golden up-sweep hairdo, Nathan thought she looked like a queen. His hand covered hers on top of the table. They gazed into each others' eyes and their souls met on that mystic plain where two souls meet and become one. Their hearts melted into each other '*like a running brook that sings its melody to the night. Like the strings of a lute that quiver with the same music.'*

-Kahlil Gibran-

XXX

It was a spring wedding. The Houston weather was perfect. Azaleas filled the landscape. The house was filled with tulips, gladiolus and even lilacs had been flown in from Ohio, because they were grandmother Vista's favorite.

Ruby had been flown in for the wedding. She looked out of place with all the fancy ladies and wedding trimmings. She stayed close to Vista, putting leftovers in the shopping bag she carried. Ruby was disappointed that Vista still did not remember her.

Because Nickoel was Catholic and Nathan was Jewish they decided to have a garden wedding.

They stood under a canopy of flowers for the ceremony and under a huge cake in the form of an arch to greet their guests. A white ladder trimmed with flowers and ribbons stood ready to accommodate the couple as they climbed up to the top of the arch to cut their wedding cake.

Nickoel and Nathan looked so radiant, they took on an ethereal countenance. Their eyes met and clung and the birds seemed to quit their chirping as the minister read, *'You were born together and together you shall be forever more'—Kahlil Gibran*

As the service ended baby Andy let out a cry. "Bring the baby to me." Vista ordered.

Ruby ran to tell the Elias' that Greta was asking for baby Andy. She refused to call Vista anything but Greta. The Elias's ran to Vista, hoping that if she remembered the baby she would remember them.

"Give me little Andy. He is sleepy." They placed Vista's wheelchair in the corner where the sun was streaming in and she sang to little Andy. She did not remember the Elias'.

Nickoel and Nathan did not take a long Honeymoon. They wanted to be near the family. They decided they would go to Los Angeles and stay in the mansion on the mountain that now belonged to grandmother.

They would see to it that Ruby got back to her neighborhood. Now Ruby was the proud owner of a condo by the park. It was all furnished and an attorney was appointed to see to it that she should never want for anything. The attorney Sam Golden had called Nathan complaining that his charge still insisted on pushing her cart in the park and begging on the Hollywood streets.

Ruby had been married once to a professor. She had been his student in geology. He was older and died when Ruby was entering middle age. She was still healthy and she had always dreamed of prospecting for precious stones. She traveled from Africa to the mountains and jungles of South America in the search of stones. She found some, just enough to keep her interested until her money ran out. She had no family and the professor's family never did have anything to do with her. She had it in her mind that she did not want or deserve Social Security. Loneliness can make people act in strange ways. So Ruby, with her new found wealth, still preferred the streets of Hollywood.

CHAPTER THIRTEEN
What To Do With Mother Vista

Several months had passed since Vista was found in Los Angeles. She had regained her weight but the sparkle had left her eyes. She spoke often of her childhood in the Hocking hills of Ohio. She still called Nickoel, Esther. The Conrads' had hired a woman to stay with her. They did not want to go through the turmoil of losing her again.

Her friends from church came to see her and never came back again. Her long time friend Sylvia asked, "What are you going to do with her? This is a lot of responsibility for the family."

"What do you suggest we do? Hide her away somewhere."

Nickoel said tears brimming in her eyes. "Grandmother was always there for us. We love her still. I will take care of her." she said in a nasty tone.

"I didn't mean . . ." Sylvia did not finish. She picked up her purse and headed for the door, but not before they heard her mumble, "My dear friend, she might as well be dead."

Nickoel started to go after Sylvia. Her Mother caught her arm and held her. "What are you going to do, Nickoel? Hit the old woman?" Esther asked.

"Yes! I wanted to strike her. She is so hateful to say such a thing." Nickoel ran to her room.

Esther sat down in the breakfast nook and cried. Her poor mother, who had always been the center of things, was now a passive child. She looked into the living room and watched as Vista rocked one of Nickoel's old dolls. She would rock and sing for hours. Sometimes she sang the same song over and over.

Nickoel and Nathan had their own apartment but Nickoel spent most of her free time close to Mother Vista. She was so sure she would regain her memory and call her by her name. Nathan complained that Nickoel was spending too much time with her grandmother.

It was Christmas time. Nickoel remembered the great times her and grandmother Vista had shopping at the Galleria. She tried to get Vista interested. Nothing, just blank stares and lately she had gotten abusive. She would strike out at Nickoel for no reason.

It was breaking Nickoel's heart. She had lost weight since her wedding and it was of great concern to Nathan and the family.

One evening Nickoel had to work late at the office. Nathan took the opportunity to bring a Doctor friend of his to talk to the family.

Doctor Jordan examined Vista and turned to the family. "She is never going to get any better. She will steadily get worse. This is very difficult for the family and loved ones. But you must understand, Vista does not know or care where she is or with whom. She would be just as happy with strangers as family. I know this is difficult for all of you to accept. She may have lucid moments, but she will sink back into that mental chasm of no return." Doctor Mark Jordan explained.

"What should we do?" Esther asked.

"Like I said, she has no sense of where she is or who she is or who you are. She is like a child who only needs to be clean and well fed. She could cause those caring for her to become ill. It is very wearing on the mind and body to take care of a family member in this condition. I suggest you check out the nursing homes in the vicinity."

Nickoel had came in and was standing in the doorway of the living room. A look of disbelief was on her face.

"And who's great idea was this? Grandmother is not going anywhere. I'll quit work if I have to, but I will take care of her."

Father Conrad spoke up. He usually left all the decisions to others, but this was different. He seemed taller as he spoke. Like the military man he used to be. His shoulders were squared and he spoke in a brash manner. "I don't believe this is your decision to make young lady. Your grandmother, is Esther and my responsibility. You have a husband to take care of. We will do what we think best. Now you go home with your husband." Esther looked surprised.

"This is your doing, Nathan. If they put Grandmother in a home I will never forgive you." She ran from the house and her car wheels screeched as she spun out of the drive.

"She must have been very close to her grandmother." Doctor Jordan ventured.

"Sometimes I think too close." Esther said.

"I heard about all the trouble you have had with your Mother, Mrs. Conrad. Nathan was telling me the story and it is quite a story. I can't imagine her getting married when she didn't even know her name. She must have been some lady in her day. Remember what

I told you. Maybe you could hire someone to stay with her all the time. They have to be watched like children. It is very wearing on the family to watch her die a little more day by day." Doctor Jordan said.

"A nursing home gets you away from that for a while."

"We will think about what you have told us Doctor Jordan. Thank you for coming." Father Conrad said.

"I've got to go to Nickoel. I know there is going to be a terrible scene. She is so protective of grandmother Vista." Nathan hung his head as though he had already lost the battle.

Father Conrad poured himself a cup of coffee and sat down at the kitchen table. "Don't cry Esther you have been a good, faithful and loving daughter. These things happen. Life has been good to your mother, until now. She has had lots more to love and to love her. Her life was fuller than her friend Sylvias. Try to think of the positive side, Esther".

The next week on Nickoel's day off she insisted on going alone and taking grandmother to the Galleria Christmas shopping. She would wheel her around in the wheel chair that the Galleria provided for shoppers.

Only Nickoel was not going shopping. She had been given the job of taking care of Vista's banking and was in charge of her checking and savings which gave her plenty money to do with as she pleased. She bought first class tickets on TWA for Los Angeles. She even had a limousine waiting to take them to the mountain mansion. Nickoel was kidnaping her grandmother Vista.

Nickoel knew it would not take the family long to figure out where they had gone. If the family saw how much it meant to her, to be close to grandmother Vista, they may change their minds.

She would hire a nurse to stay with them around the clock. She had the gardener and house keeper already. They would have the house ready for their arrival.

Nickoel had called ahead and asked Cecil Anthony to buy a hospital bed, wheelchair and special electric lounge chair for Vista. Nickoel would get a nutritionist and have a doctor prescribe the best vitamins for grandmother. The fresh mountain and sea air would do a lot for Vista. She would nurse her back to health, she would!

Father Conrad was the first to call. "Are you both all right?" He asked. "Be careful of the cliff side of the house. That is a steep drop off."

"I know Daddy. Cecil has already built a high wall around the patio. You are not angry with me? How about Mama?"

"No Nickoel. But you must realize grandmother is getting old and she is sick. You are going to have to be ready to let go." Father Conrad said.

"Not yet, Daddy. She is going to get better. Just wait and see.'

"And what about Nathan? He is very upset and broken hearted."

"He can wait, if he loves me. Grandmother has so little time left. I want to be near her. Make him understand, Daddy."

"I'll do my best, dear. Goodnight. Call us if you need anything."

Nickoel hung up and a twinge of homesickness churned her stomach and put an ache in her heart. She watched as grandmother Vista rocked and sang to her old doll. How she longed for the old days when they laughed at each other's antics, over their morning coffee. She took her coffee out to the patio and felt closed in. The high wall that Cecil had built spoiled the view of the valley below. She went back to the breakfast nook and looked out over the vast valley and wished that Nathan would come to her.

That evening just as she put away the supper dishes the front doorbell rang. There stood Nathan, a happy smile curled his lips. "I thought you might be missing your husband." Nickoel ran into his outstretched arms.

"Oh! Nathan. I need you so much." After they both stopped crying she asked about his job.

"Remember the company that bought my first computer chip order? Now I am working as vice president of the Monroe Computer Company here in Los Angeles. You just have to be able to accept change when you are rising in the business world. Mother Vista is not getting better is she?"

"Not yet. The dietitian gave me a special diet for her and we walk every day. If her mind were as good as her body, it would be wonderful. I hate having to lock her in her room at night, but I am afraid she will wonder off again."

"I know baby. That's why I came to help you."

That night after Nickoel helped Vista with her bath and put her to bed she came back to find Nathan in front of a roaring fire with a bottle of Dom and two crystal glasses.

"To celebrate my new job." he said as he reached for Nickoel and switched off the lights leaving only the light from the fireplace to throw shadows across the room. Nickoel felt safe and happy as she snuggled close to Nathan and felt his strong hairy arms enfold her.

Next morning they walked arm in arm to the end of the drive where Nathan had left the rental car. "Good luck Darling, have a happy day. Oh dear! I got that from Grandmother, that's what she always said."

"And will again." Nathan said.

When Nickoel returned to the kitchen she found all the pots and pans and pan lids strewn around the kitchen floor. She tried to pick them up and grandmother Vista shoved her up against the refrigerator. It took Nickoel by surprise and she began to cry.

"Don't cry Esther. You look so ugly when you cry."

"Grandmother, I am Nickoel."

"Are we going Christmas shopping at the Galleria?"

Nickoel was so excited that Grandmother Vista had remembered the Galleria that she stopped crying. But when she tried to hug her, Vista pushed her away.

Nickoel backed off and as she replaced all the pans she explained to her that they would go shopping the next day.

That evening Nathan held her close as she cried while telling him of the pan incident.

The next day the nurse had been busy on the second floor and Nickoel came into the kitchen to find flour, corn meal and syrup poured all about the kitchen. Nickoel had been writing a long letter to her mother, back in Texas.

It took Nickoel a long time to put the kitchen to rights. She decided not to tell Nathan. He would suggest again that they put her grandmother in an institution. She decided somethings would be better to keep to herself.

It was now spring. The shrubs were flowering and this day grandmother had named everyone of them. Vista had gained a little weight and seemed better. Last evening she had baked a cake from scratch.

Nickoel was so proud of her. Then at dinner, Vista picked up her salad fork and threw it at Nathan. It hit his glass of wine, spilling the purple contents onto the white cloth. He was so astonished that he didn't know what to say. He left the table and went to the study. Nickoel did not follow because she did not know how she could justify grandmother Vista's actions.

After she had bathed and put her to bed, locking the door behind her, she went to Nathan hating the scene that she knew would follow.

"Can't you see she needs to be put away?. She is becoming a menace." He said in a stern voice.

"That is the first time she has ever done that."

"Yes, but there are many other things you have not told me. The nurse keeps me informed of what is taking place here, the spills and broken dishes. And look at you, you are not the pretty young girl I married. You look like an old hag. You have lost too much weight. You never dress up anymore. That old lady is robbing you of your youth and me of my once beautiful wife. I am beginning to resent her more everyday. I can't help it." He left the room and went to his bedroom slamming the door.

A day would start out cheerful. Then the clouds would close over again and it would be a bad day. Vista began to balk at going into the dining room, and once there would refuse to eat. She would get a gleam in her eye and pick up her plate and try to throw it. "I can break the plate if I want to." Nickoel had gotten very quick at judging her grandmother's moods and being able to grab the plates before she could let them fly. Nathan never intervened. He started taking his plate to the glassed-in solarium that overlooked the valley. Nickoel wished she could join him there and watch the sunset but she would not leave her grandmother until she was in bed for the night. That too was a chore. No matter how many requests Nickoel had anticipated, there would always be something else she would demand before retiring, a glass of warm milk, water, an extra pillow.

By the time she got her grandmother to bed she was too tired to be good company to her neglected husband.

Nickoel knew she was not being a good wife. But all she could think of were the great times she and her grandmother had spent over the years. She knew too, that she would lose her soon and every moment was precious even if the quality of their relationship had dissipated. As they walked along, hand in hand, Nickoel thought of Kahlil Gibran's, *The Prophet,* and his verses on death. *And what is it to cease breathing, but to free the breath from its restless tides, that it may rise and expand and seek God unencumbered? For life and death are one, even as the river and the sea are one.* A breeze from the sea blew across Nickoel's face and she felt a chill in the midmorning sun. She held Grandmother's hand tight, not wanting to ever let her go.

Someday she would have to let go . . . but not yet.

CHAPTER FOURTEEN

Grandmother's Last Sunset

It was a hot, sticky, August morning. Not a leaf stirred as Nickoel studied the stranger in her mirror, a face she hardly recognized. Huge black circles underlined her tired eyes. She looked dissipated. She woke up tired and went to bed tired.

Nathan left every morning before she awakened. It seemed he was coming home later every evening. Many nights she was already asleep before he arrived. He said his new job was more exacting, that he had to work late at the office to catch up. It crossed her mind that he may have someone else. Looking in the mirror, she would not be surprised. Who would want to come home to a washed out woman, who looked old beyond her years?

Nathan was such a handsome man, with pleasant mannerisms. Any woman would be taken by his charming ways. She pictured him sucking on his cold pipe, a dark unruly curl falling unto his forehead, as he pondered over some business problem.

Nickoel heard a thud coming from Mother Vista's room. She ran in, to find nurse Elaine sitting on the floor. Vista had caught her off balance as she tried to dress her. Vista had pushed hard, knocking her to the floor. "You crazy old woman. You should be put away." She screamed at Vista. Vista had struck out at her once too often.

"I'll finish dressing her. Go to the kitchen. I want to talk to you." Nickoel said, her voice brisk and cross.

"There is nothing to talk about. I quit. And if you had any sense you would give it up too. She needs more professional help than we can give. Send me my check."

Before Nickoel could finish dressing Mother Vista, she heard nurse Elaine's car leave the drive.

Nickoel had no tears left to cry. She took her Grandmother to the kitchen and made her breakfast,

Vista had refused to go for her morning walk anymore. She only wanted to sit in the rocker and sing to Nickoel's old baby doll. She had not said a single word for several weeks. She never answered when Nickoel talked to her. She just stared into space and rocked back and forth. Nathan and Nickoel were growing apart. It had been weeks since she had felt his arms around her. The only affection he showed, was a peck on the cheek when he left for the office.

Nickoel was very tired. It was all she could do to get through the day. She was alone with Vista except for the maid who came in twice a week.

As Nickoel took the doll away from her grandmother's arm, she said. "Where is baby Andy? I want to hold him."

Her voice startled Nickoel, She had not heard her Grandmother speak in weeks.

"I'll call for him, Grandmother." She tried to hug Vista, but she pushed her away. "I want baby Andy."

Nickoel ran to the phone and called the Elias'. Detective Andy Elias had just gotten home from the late night shift. "We'll be there within the hour." He told Nickoel. They had kept in touch and knew this was the first time Vista had asked for the baby since the wedding in Houston.

"My little Andy." Vista said as she held him close. The baby was almost a year old now. He hugged and kissed her and said, "mam maw wist". He could not articulate Vista.

"I love you." Vista crooned. "You will grow up to be a doctor someday. Esther, when you sell the farm, I want baby Andy to have money for college. You understand?" Vista said loud and clear.

"Yes, Grandmother, of course. Whatever you say." Nickoel did not tell her that the farm in the Hocking Hills of Ohio had been sold many years before and that she had gone to Texas to live. It didn't matter. Mr. Farley had left Vista a lot of money. Nickoel would see to it that Andy would get enough for his education. She was remembering how they had taken care of her grandmother when she was lost.

The Elias' stayed most of the day. Captain Andy slept on the sofa in the solarium. Vista sang and rocked the baby and watched him while he napped.

Vista ate lunch at the table with Alice and Andy. She listened intently to the conversation and even broke in a few times to express her own feelings and opinions.

Nickoel was elated. Finally a break through.

Grandmother Vista was herself again, except she still called Nickoel by her mother's name, Esther.

That night as Nickoel helped her dress for bed, she allowed Nickoel to hug and kiss her. Just to smell the faint aroma of her perfume, made Nickoel so happy that she began to cry.

"Don't cry Esther. Tomorrow we will go shopping at the Galleria. You always liked the Galleria."

"Yes, Grandmother." Nickoel did not try to explain to her that they were not in Houston, but atop a mountain near Los Angeles.

"After we shop we will take a ride to the Hocking Hills. I want to check on the farm. I haven't been there in a long time. Fall is such a lovely time in the hills. The dogwoods will be red and all the trees will be gold and yellow, and the pumpkins will be ripe. We will bring back some for jack-o-lanterns. There hasn't been a frost yet has there, Esther?"

"No, Mother." Nickoel did not remind her that she was Nickoel and not her daughter, Esther, or that this was the middle of August, not late September. She did not want to say anything that would cause her Grandmother to withdraw, back into that mental chasm that she could not share.

Nickoel was happier than she had been in a long time. As she tucked Vista into bed, She pulled Nickoel down and kissed her. She even let her nuzzle her neck as she whispered. "I love you Grandmother."

"I love you too, Esther."

Nickoel closed the door softly. She did not lock it as she usually did. She went to the phone and called her mother in Houston.

"It's only temporary dear. Don't expect too much. Tomorrow, she will have forgotten all about today."

But the next morning she was still rational and asked for bacon and eggs and English muffins.

Just as Nickoel was about to set the table for breakfast the doorbell rang. It was Aunt Dolly. She had driven down from San Francisco to bring Vista the portrait she had just finished of her. Aunt Dolly was a marvelous artist.Her brilliant colors and the vibrant expressions of her portraits were very pleasing.

Vista recognized Dolly and called her by name. As they enjoyed a leisurely breakfast, Vista reached over and patted Dolly's hand. "You're pregnant aren't you?"

Dolly looked surprised. "I don't know. I did miss my period this month, but that has happened before."

"You're pregnant. My baby girl is going to have a golden haired little girl." Vista said emphatically.

That in itself would be unusual since Aunt Dolly was olive complexioned with big black eyes and dark hair. Nickoel had heard stories of grandmother's predictions on pregnancy. Her daughters would laugh because their mother always knew they were pregnant before they did.

Dolly had a business luncheon in San Francisco. She was being commissioned to paint a mural on the walls of City Hall.

After Dolly left, Vista went to her room to rest. Nickoel rested in the white wicker chair in the corner of the solarium that looked for miles, out over the valley below. She heard Nathan's car and ran to meet him. This was unexpected. He never came home in the middle of the day.

"We need to talk." he said, as he threw his keys on the hall table.

Nickoel felt a cold chill run through her body. He was going to tell her, there was someone else. He came to ask for a divorce. They went to the solarium. As she looked out over the valley, she thought how quick a sunny day can turn to clouds. She sat down because her trembling legs would not hold her. She felt sick. Her stomach lurched and she had to hold on tight to keep from fainting.

Nathan started talking in a calm but deadly voice. His voice escalated as he spoke. He was explaining that he had found a home close by, that would take Vista during the day and return her at dinner time. This would give Nickoel a respite from the twenty four hour days that was draining her strength, physically and mentally.

"But she would be among strangers. She would feel lost. She talked to Aunt Dolly today. She held little Andy yesterday. She even spoke of giving baby Andy money for his education. She's better Nathan. She is!" Her voice escalated as well, and she began to cry.

"I come home to a wife, I don't know anymore. I love you Nicky. I just don't know how much more of this I can endure."

In the heat of the argument, they did not hear the front door open and close. Nickoel got up, her knees were still shaking. She went to the kitchen and placed the tea kettle on the stove. As Andy came in, the kettle began to whistle. She pulled it off quickly, hoping the whistle had not awakened Vista.

"Will you see if the tea pot woke up grandmother please, Nathan" She was not sure she could make it to her room without fainting. She hated arguments and this one had left her drained.

"She is not in her room." Nathan said in a worried tone.

"Did you look in her bathroom?"

"Yes. She is not here."

"Oh my God! She's gone again!" With new found strength, Nickoel ran from room to room calling for her. Her adrenaline pumping, she ran to the patio. Cecil had mowed the lawn yesterday, maybe he forgot to close the gate to the patio, that led out to a high cliff. The gate was locked. Neither of them spoke. They went to the car and drove down the mountain side.

"Nathan! Where could she have gone. I thought she was napping. It's my fault. I left her door unlocked."

Nathan patted her hand. "Don't worry, she could not have gone far. We will find her."

Maybe she fell down the mountain. Maybe . . . It's so hot today, the radio said 93 degrees." Nickoel wailed. As they neared the foot of the mountain they saw her ahead.

Vista's face was red and perspiration beaded her brow. Her clothes were wet through with perspiration. Nickoel hugged her gently. Vista did not push her away.

"My little Nickoel. My golden haired Nickoel. I've been looking everywhere for you. Nathan looked surprised. He caught her as she fainted and carried her to the car.

"Nathan, she said my name. She knows me."

The doctor came and said she had a stroke, and she was very weak. Her heart was wearing out and there was no use taking her to the hospital, as she would not make it.

Just as the sun was setting in all its glory, Vista opened her eyes and looked at Nickoel. She smiled a weary smile as she drew her last breath. Grandmother Vista was the other side of a heartbeat.

Nathan was holding Nickoel and Nickoel was hugging her grandmother Vista. They sat there for a long time. The after-glow of the sunset painted the horizon in bright hues of pinks, oranges and purple. As they viewed the sunset Nickoel said: "Grandmother Vista is on her way to Heaven."

"Yes, Nickoel. And you my love were faithful to the end. I shall love only you, all my life." Nickoel turned to Nathan. As he cradled her in his arms he said; *"Nor, in truth, would the honors of illustrious women continue after death, if their own spirits did not make us preserve a longer remembrance of them."*—*De Senectute, XXII*

THE END

CPSIA information can be obtained
at www.ICGtesting.com
Printed in the USA
LVHW090727280223
740505LV00004B/629